911

First Responders

at

Ground Zero

By David M. Bresnahan

(Black and White Version)

911 First Responders at Ground Zero

PRINTING HISTORY
First Edition October 2001
Published as "9-11 Terror in America"
ISBN: 188163695X

Second Revised Edition, color version March 2018
Published as "911 First Responders at Ground Zero"
Revised and re-published by the author.
ISBN-13: 978-1533593054
ISBN-10: 1533593051

Second Revised Edition, black and white version March 2018 (this edition)
Published as "911 First Responders at Ground Zero"
Revised and re-published by the author, black and white version.
ISBN 10: 1986515273
ISBN 13: 9781986515276

Permission and information requests:
David M. Bresnahan, Box 1396, Sandy, UT 84091-1396
Dave@Bresnahan.org

.

Table of Contents

DEDICATION

I would like to dedicate this book to all the first responders, who I consider to be the dispatchers, emergency medical service personnel, police, fire, military, volunteer bystanders, and all rescue workers who responded to the tragedy on 911. Some sacrificed their lives that day, others died at a later time because of injuries and illnesses they incurred, and others continue to suffer.

This book is also dedicated to the many thousands of people who died or were injured on 911, and to their families and loved ones. It is also dedicated to the many, many victims who were impacted by physical or emotional injury.

We have learned a great deal from the response to the attacks on that fateful day. First responders have learned from the challenges faced by those who struggled to find survivors at Ground Zero. This book is also dedicated to the many first responders and military who respond at a moment's notice when an emergency or disaster occurs today.

ACKNOWLEDGMENT

This book exists because of the courageous people who were willing to be interviewed just days after the attacks on 9-11. They understood my desire to record for history what it was like to be there, on the ground at Ground Zero in New York City during those first 24 hours. George Sleigh was the first person I spoke to. He was reluctant, but then agreed to permit me to interview him and to use his story to enable us all to see through his eyes the events that took place on September 11, 2001. He was most likely the last person out of the north tower before it collapsed.

George's story is heart-touching and eye-opening, giving us all a much more accurate perception of what it was like to escape from the north tower, only to be immersed and surrounded by unimaginable scenes of terror and destruction.

I then began the process of locating other people who were there, and many of them generously shared what is a very personal experience in an effort to help establish this historical record. Each is a hero. Each is an example of the heroism this event brought forth from so many others during those first 24 hours.

And so a very special "thank you" goes to George Sleigh, William Cahill, Timothy Hubbard, James Fenn, Maurice Ottolia, Brian Bliss, and Pat O'Flaherty. William Cahill contributed many photos included in the book, for which I am most grateful. Each played an important role, and by sharing their stories they have given us a more complete picture of the monumental task that they and so many others rose to the challenge to perform. They represent the many, many people from all walks of life who participated in the rescue effort. Through their eyes we have a glimpse of what it was like to be there. Part of that picture comes, too, from the photographs taken by William Cahill that he generously gave permission to use in this book.

Grateful acknowledgment goes to Lowell Ponte, former Reader's Digest Roving Editor, an artist with words whose expert editing skillfully polished this work. A special thank you goes to Jennifer Reed, my virtual assistant from SecretaryZone.com who helped to format this second edition of the book.

I would also like to acknowledge the patience and understanding of my wife and young children, who endured the long weeks without me while this book was being completed.

Most especially, all who are associated with this book acknowledge the need to thank God. We acknowledge the many blessings that have come in spite of this disaster, and we acknowledge His guidance in the completion of this project.

May God bless America, and may God bless us all.

PREFACE

This is the second printing of this book which was originally published just two months after the terrible tragedy on September 11, 2001 under the title of 9-11 Terror in America. That first edition was published by Dwight Wallington owner of Windsor House Publishing. This first printing sold out, and then sadly the company was disbanded when Dwight passed away. Over the years I have been asked by many people to make it available once again. Other projects have kept me from doing that, until now. I decided to make it available to as many people as possible and as inexpensively as possible through e-book online, which will hopefully make this book easily available to the widest audience.

My interest at the time I wrote the book was the same as it is now, to preserve history, and to tell stores of heroes not found elsewhere. This book contains accounts of what happened at Ground Zero in New York City during the first 24 hours after the attack on the World Trade Center. Most of the news reports focused on what happened, but not on the heroic efforts being made by first responders, and average citizens who responded to the call and need for help. The interviews that make up this book are examples of the many, many unintentional heroes of that day.

I did not have control over the first publication of the book. There are changes in this printing, which are made because of additional information which became available after the first publication of this book.

Here is the Preface as it appeared in the first edition:

My wife had that look that told me something was very wrong. She struggled to control her emotions as she told me, "You better come see what's happened." I came in the room and was astonished by what was showing on the television. However, I was in a hurry. I was leaving on a flight and had to get to the airport. Just over an hour later I was in line to board my flight when the announcement was made that all flights were cancelled.

I was watching the coverage on the television in the airline terminal, and I remember thinking "why isn't anyone talking about terrorism," because it seemed obvious to me. The first thing that came to my mind was terrorism. I remembered a discussion I had with Sen. Robert Bennett (R.-Utah) on New Year's Eve of Y2K. He was at the Emergency Management Center in the State Capital. I was there as a member of the press, and we were all waiting to see if computer systems everywhere would melt down.

The night passed. The sun rose. Nothing went wrong. Journalists were quickly trying to find something to write about when the only story was that there was no story. Bennett and I discussed the threat of terrorism and some of the training and drills going on within many government agencies.

"It's not a matter of if, it's a matter of when," he told me in a very serious tone. He also said he knew that a number of attempts to attack us had already been prevented, but that sooner or later a group of terrorists would succeed and do something really bad.

His comments came as no surprise. The threat of terrorism using weapons of mass destruction was already known to me. As a reporter I had done investigative articles about not only the potential threat but also the preparations being made by the military and other government agencies to deal with those threats.

On September 30, 1998, I reported on Osama bin Laden's deadly plans to attack the United States. I was criticized for doing this and labeled an alarmist. A former CIA employee who knew I was working on terrorism threats called to say he had a fax I should see.

It was sent by Osama bin Laden to his soldiers all over the world. "He's giving them their marching orders.

You'll want to see this," he said. "I'm giving this to a few good reporters. Do you want me to fax it to you?"

Naturally I wanted it, but when I told my publisher about it he was unhappy. My source needed protection and could not be revealed. He had been reliable and would be needed for future stories. Giving his name would hurt his business and would certainly eliminate him as a potential future source.

After newspapers in London and Jerusalem came out with stories about the fax, he let me include information about it buried in another article. Two days later my publisher agreed to let me mention the fax in a somewhat related story.

When I spoke to official sources from the FBI regarding the threat posed by Osama bin Laden, I was told that this millionaire Saudi Svengali was regarded as a madman with a bark bigger than his bite. The FBI did not want a copy of my fax and would not say if they had already seen it. They told me bin Laden was incapable of carrying out the goals of the fax.

The fax was purportedly intercepted as it went to 5,000 or more soldiers stationed in groups or cells all around the world, including some within the U.S. The translation of the apparently Arabic writing on the fax was written in between the lines by someone. It never told his "soldiers" what specific targets to attack, but it stated goals for attacks on U.S. interests. The fax did not say how to accomplish the goals, nor did it specify a day or hour to strike.

According to the fax, the attacks should:
- Bring commercial airlines to a halt
- Stop all maritime traffic
- Occupy U.S. embassies around the world
- Shut down U.S. banking

Three years later bin Laden appeared on his way to accomplishing his goals, despite the assurance of intelligence sources at the time of his fax that this was impossible.

For the first time in history, every commercial flight in the U.S. was grounded, along with most international flights. The financial markets were all closed, and financial crunch began that impacted not only the U.S. but most other countries as well.

All those I interviewed for this book said they expect future attacks on U.S. soil. Polls show that a majority of Americans also believe that more attacks are coming. People are preparing for emergencies by acquiring things far beyond extra food and water for 72-hour survival kits. One week after the attacks of September 11th, a survey found that military surplus gas masks could not be purchased at any price. All inventories were exhausted within days of the attacks.

My intelligence sources have told me for several years that we are under a very real threat of attacks by terrorists using weapons of mass destruction. These attacks, they expect, will come sooner or later - without warning. We are also being targeted by relentless cyber-attacks that could disrupt the computers that are the central nervous system of our telephones, financial transactions, and Internet communications worldwide. Such attacks can kill our computer systems in much the same way nerve gas kills people.

Other possible attacks include the use of chemical and biological weapons that can be sprayed in the air or placed in our water supplies, or destruction of key power plants and communication systems. Bin Laden is now gone, but the terrorists he inspired could easily accomplish most if not all such goals. What once seemed to be the ravings of a madman are now stark and real dangers.

Therefore, I felt no surprise when images of the first attack on the World Trade Center tower appeared on television. It was a shock, but not surprise. This was, I knew instantly, the work of a terrorist group. Then suddenly the second plane hit, and my shock turned to anger that we failed to prevent this horrible tragedy.

But then, just as suddenly, my thoughts turned to what must be going on at what we soon would call "Ground Zero." The pictures on television were not bringing us the horror that must certainly be taking place around, and inside those towers. In my mind I was trying to visualize the death and destruction that had already taken place, along with the panic of those left alive. My thoughts: What must it be like? What about the people in the towers above and below the floors where the plane hit? Will they get out? I didn't like the probable answers.

The call went out for help, and police and firefighters as well as National Guard within reach of New York sped to the scene. They knew help would be urgently needed, and they were ready and willing to do whatever was asked of them.

This book is an effort to give some perspective to this horrific tragedy by seeing it through the eyes of people who were right there at Ground Zero in the first 24 hours. During that time most of us only saw what television was able to show us – from a distance. The media was not allowed in, and because of that what we learned from it was limited.

We can get no closer than to hear personally from the last survivor to escape from one of the towers. George Sleigh actually watched out his 91st floor window as the first plane slammed into the north tower just a few feet above him. His story of how he got all his office staff down the stairs and out just as the first tower collapsed is dramatic and inspirational.

As Sleigh was racing down the stairs in an hour-long struggle to escape, firefighters were rushing in. More than 300 police and firemen gave their lives in a valiant effort to save other lives. The stories of what they did will touch your heart, remind you how precious life is, and deepen your awareness of the selfless goodness of these heroes.

Each of the first responders interviewed in this book offers a perspective to those of us who were there in our hearts and prayers, but not physically, to see and experience for ourselves through their stories. But just as they provide perspective to us, we have a perspective and knowledge base they did not have.

Watching on television gave most of us the 'big picture,' the overall view of the situation and what was going on. Those like George Sleigh had no idea what was happening beyond their own very confined surroundings. Many of the rescue workers describe events, but could not give details other than what they personally observed.

And so this book contains the impressions and experiences of a number of people involved in this enormous tragedy. It makes no attempt to provide details beyond what was seen and heard through the senses of those who were there.

If this were a news article, I as a reporter would attempt to bring together information from various sources and combine that with timelines and other information resources to provide detailed explanations and factual data for a complete story. This book instead records the actual words and experiences of those involved – their perceptions of what was going on around them, their feelings, and their reactions.

When a rescuer, for example, describes various buildings there is no attempt to identify the specific building. The rescuers all expressed confusion about their locations and the names of specific buildings and streets. They also were unable to identify many other workers they spent time with. They worked together as brothers without even knowing each other's names. Strangers came from other states and found themselves working next to buildings they couldn't identify. And when a few survivors were found alive, the rescuers were filled with joy even though they did not know so much as the name of the person who is alive today because of them.

As a journalist I could add to their knowledge about such details through my research, but I did not. Instead I decided to let them tell their own stories in their own voices, from their perspectives. After all the interviews, it became obvious that plenty of news reports have documented the hard, cold facts but missed some of the basic human stories that went unseen.

This book instead lets these soft, warm human beings who lived through the horrible events have their say. Most are telling their stories publicly for the first time. And through them you can touch some of what they experienced, mind to mind and heart to heart.

They did not come to me to tell their story. I had to seek out each of them and ask for their help with this project. Each was anxious not to be held up as a hero or someone special. They wanted to go on with life with no special attention to their participation in this event. Each had to be convinced that their story represented many other stories that the American people, indeed the people of the world needed to know in order to fully understand what happened and what it was like in those first 24 hours.

In my effort to tell the story of the experiences at Ground Zero I am in no way minimizing what happened at the Pentagon or at the crash site in Pennsylvania. Perhaps witnesses to those events will make their stories known as well.

My life has been forever changed by interviewing the people for this book. They enabled me to see, hear, and experience a part of what it was like for them to deal with this attack. Now it is my job to convey this to you so that you can also gain a more human perspective of this event.

If, God forbid, more such attacks are to come, then what we can learn from those who tell their stories here may be key to our survival, both as individuals and as a nation. Theirs are the qualities of intelligence, courage, compassion, cooperation, determination, and love that made them survivors – or willing to make sacrifices so others could survive. From their personal stories, many of you could become inoculated against the terror with which terrorists aim to infect America and the world.

I agree with what President George W. Bush said. We feel horror at what was done on September 11th, but we should not feel terror. The terrorists use fear as a weapon, knowing it can be contagious. But courage and goodness and love can also spread by example from one person to another, which is what Christ taught. By reading this book, you can "catch" the best virtues of those you will meet in these pages and their examples will change you.

The people I interviewed have a common trait. Each of them expressed a deep faith in God. They came from a variety of denominations and levels of faith prior to the attacks. Facing Ground Zero, they all turned to God, and here share with us some very personal feelings. Men with reputations as big, tough, no nonsense cops were very open about their grief. Some spoke of their already-strong faith and how it sustained them. Others said they had renewed or increased their faith as a result of what happened.

My own faith has been strong for many years. I had an Irish Catholic father and a Swedish Protestant mother who taught me good Christian values that led to me becoming a member of The Church of Jesus Christ of Latter-day Saints. I am grateful that I know God lives. Jesus is indeed the Christ, the true Son of God. I know that God hears and answers prayer, and I'm grateful for His plan of salvation and the Restored Gospel of Jesus Christ. My faith strengthens me in the face of adversity.

I am strengthened as I realize we are all a child of God, struggling to do our best in this life of challenge and difficulties. People of many faiths united in prayer in the days, weeks, and months following 9-11. Regardless of specific denomination, people throughout the world were united and our combined faith helped us all to heal.

This tragedy, horrible as it is, has moved many people to seek what has been missing in their lives.

Chapter 1

Last Man Out?

George Sleigh stood at the 91st floor window of his office in the World Trade Center's north tower and watched as American Airlines Flight 11 crashed into the floors directly above him. There was no time for panic. Sleigh calmly shouted to his fellow employees to get under their desks.

An instant later the ceiling and a wall came crashing in. All the employees, fortunately, were safe beneath their desks, safe, at least, for the moment.

Sleigh and his fellow employees were alive, but Sleigh knew he had to get them out of the building fast. His mind flashed back to 1993, when he helped evacuate people from the 106th floor of the south tower. A terrorist bomb had exploded in its parking structure. If the explosive-laden vehicle had been parked against a key pillar, demolition experts later calculated, its detonation could have toppled the entire tower into Manhattan – killing all inside and thousands more where it fell.

His evacuation down 106 flights of stairs physically challenged Sleigh in 1993. Now 63 years old and in declining health, he would have to make that stressful scramble for safety again. Without consciously thinking about it, he sensed that his life depended on going down all those stairs once more.

"My legs hurt for weeks," he said of the experience in 1993, but that memory did not slow him from what he now had to do to save himself and the others in his office.

Sleigh is a naval architect for American Bureau of Shipping, a company founded in New York City in 1862. The main office is now in Houston, Texas. That day only 12 of the 22 Manhattan employees were in the office. No one else was on the floor because all its other offices were vacant.

Sometimes bad news turns out to be a blessing. ABS's offices used to be on the 106th floor of the other WTC tower, but a budget tightening in late 1999 downsized them to a smaller, less expensive office space on the 91st floor of the north tower. The first plane crashed into the floors just above that 91st floor, narrowly missing Sleigh and his office mates. The second plane hit the south tower and most likely would have trapped or incinerated Sleigh and his co-workers had they remained in that prestigious 106th floor office.

Sleigh had not thought about fate in those moments after the crash. Only after it was over and he agreed to be interviewed from his home in New Jersey did he ponder his good fortune. Had his company not moved, or had the move been to a north tower office higher than the 91st floor, he would almost certainly have died in horror and agony as did thousands of others.

More than luck would be needed to get him out alive on September 11, 2001. Quick action and level heads were essential if Sleigh and his co-workers were to survive. No one then knew that the building would totally collapse in just one hour and 40 minutes. No one knew a second plane was soon to hit the south tower causing that to collapse in just 52 minutes. Few imagined the kind of nightmare that was unfolding. And these great steel and concrete skyscrapers where 50,000 people worked might fill with smoke from a fire, but few suspected that they could shatter into dust and twisted metal. These highest achievements of wealth and technology seemed unsinkable…like the Titanic.

Sleigh had taken Monday off (the day before the attack) and was just returning to work on Tuesday after a long weekend. He had a large workload and arrived at 7:30 a.m. Although he had a window office that faced north towards the Empire State Building, Sleigh was too busy catching up on E-mails and phone messages to admire the sunny morning view.

"At the time the plane crashed into the building I was on the phone talking to one of our other offices," said Sleigh, who had turned away from the window while he was working. Forty years earlier he had moved from his native England to find opportunity in America. He has lived here ever since.

"My office was right on the north wall of the building, looking out over the north part of the city. I was on the phone when I heard a loud roar and looked out the window. And here, almost upon us, was a plane. A large passenger plane. It was staring right at the building. It was above us and to my right, so I saw the underbelly of the plane. I noticed that the wheels were up. That kind of registered with me. All of a sudden it hit the building."

Sleigh may be one of only a handful of people who saw the plane from the level of the building where it hit and lived to tell about it. He didn't think anyone else in his office saw it other than perhaps a glimpse just at the last moment. By the time he turned and looked out the window he was only able to see the plane for only a few seconds.

"To estimate, it was two, maybe three plane lengths away at the most when I first saw it. Maybe it was farther away than that, but it was moving at a high speed," he described.

Eyewitnesses on the ground reported that both planes, just before they hit, seemed suddenly to accelerate in the direction of their targets. At least one of the planes reportedly created a sonic boom.

"It didn't seem to be (accelerating), but of course the plane was coming towards me, and most of the sound would be from the back. It didn't sound like it was increasing speed as it came toward the building, but it was so close. The thought hardly registered. Suddenly it was there," Sleigh described.

When he first looked up at the fast-approaching jetliner he felt no sudden panic or fear because he did not think the plane would hit the building.

"My first thought was crazy, but I thought, 'This guy is low.' Sometimes we see planes around the building, but they're quite a bit higher than that. And then it was into the building. I mean, it was that fast. I didn't really have time to think where he might be headed or what he was doing," Sleigh said.

During the few seconds he watched the plane, Sleigh was able to get a good view. Because the plane hit just above the 91st floor where Sleigh was working, he found himself looking at the bottom of the plane. Its right wing hit the floors directly above him. The main body of the plane impacted farther away from Sleigh, towards the middle of the building. Fuel tanks are located in the wings of planes, and these tanks were nearly full because the flight was fueled for a trip all the way to Los Angeles.

"I saw the underside of the front of the plane and one wing. I don't remember seeing an engine. I saw white and blue, and it registered in my mind as a large passenger plane. It wasn't some little two-seater. It was above me and to my right," he described.

He said he believes most if not all the people on the floors above the 91st were killed instantly or trapped when the plane hit. He knows the plane hit extremely close to his location. He believes his survival is a miracle.

"The plane was not flying level, so maybe part of it struck the same level as our floor. (Part of) the plane was above us maybe a couple floors, but where exactly it hit I'm uncertain," Sleigh said.

He had been in a previous terrorist attack on the World Trade Center in 1993, but Sleigh says it never occurred to him that the crash was anything but an accident. His description of what happens next comes from his own perception. He had no access to news reports and knew nothing about the second crash into the south tower until much later. Oddly, he was unaware that the south tower had collapsed, even though its debris nearly killed him.

"That moment (after the plane hit) was chaotic," Sleigh said. "My cubicle is up against the end partition wall of the office, and that wall kind of crumpled. All the ceiling tiles and the light fixtures came down. Books came off my book shelves. I was buried in that debris.

"One of my colleagues came rushing along to see if I was okay, and I said, 'Yes, I'm all right,' and crawled out from under. At that point I looked around. There didn't appear to be any glass broken in our office. The windows were still intact, and from what I could see the structure was still intact. There were no bent beams or anything like that. So we grouped together.

"Because of all the stuff coming down around me, I don't remember actually feeling the building move. I just heard the loud crashing. I didn't feel anything until all of this stuff started to fall down around me," said Sleigh. He says he heard no sound of an explosion during or after the crash.

"After the crash the noise stopped. It was quiet. It was relatively quiet. I couldn't hear any sound of any action going, any explosions, or any such thing as that," he explained.

As his co-workers crawled out from under the debris, they were confused about what happened. Instinct, or perhaps divine inspiration, told Sleigh to get everyone out immediately. The tendency to stand around and talk about what happened would delay their escape. Sleigh had an urgent feeling they needed to get moving.

"I think only two, maybe three people in the office perhaps saw the plane. The rest were elsewhere at that point," he explained. "I just called out, and everyone was saying, 'What happened?' I said, "Well, a plane has hit the building. Let's get out of here. We just marshaled our people. We counted heads to make sure everyone who was there was accounted for and headed down the stairs."

The only safe way out of the building was to use the stairwells, not the elevators, as everyone there had been taught. Fortunately more than one set of stairs was near their office. But before they went down Sleigh ducked back inside. He had no thought that the office would be destroyed, but he also had no idea when he would be allowed back in the building.

"In retrospect I was foolish, but my briefcase was in my office buried under the debris. Just before we left I said, 'I need my address book with my phone numbers in it.' It was in my briefcase. So I crawled back in and got that out. I mean that was only 30 seconds. I was in and out like that, and then we headed down the stairs," he explained.

"I just assumed that at some point we'd be able to get back into our office and get important documents and so on. That's the way it was after the bombing in 1993," Sleigh said of his initial expectations. He never thought the building would come down.

"The other tenants on our floor had moved out," explained Sleigh. "There was a dot com company that moved out nine months ago. They had a lot of young people. And there was a space next to us which the Port Authority donated where young artists did artwork, but none were in that day. We were the only tenants on the floor. Some other people did things there from time to time. As far as I know, everyone who was on that floor got out safely."

Two stairwells could be used to get out. The first one they tried had too much smoke, so they turned back. The next one had some smoke, but not as much, plus debris to push through. Both stairwells were empty of people because there were no people coming down from above. The power remained on, so the lights in the stairs were working, but sprinkler systems were activated and water was flowing down the stairs making them hazardous.

Sleigh took up a position at the end of his group so he would know that all members of his group were in front of him all the way down. He didn't want to have anyone fall behind. Just a couple floors below he opened a door, looked into a corridor, and saw flames. The fire from the plane's fuel had now spread downward.

"At one point I guess we were two or three floors lower. We looked down a corridor and we saw flames. They weren't in the stairwell, but we looked out into one of the doorways on one of the floors and noticed flames as we were going down," said Sleigh. He was unable to say exactly which floor he was on when he spotted the fires, but he saw no sign of people on the level that was ablaze.

At first, Sleigh's co-workers were the only people in the stairwell. No one ever joined them from higher floors. Sleigh was the slowest member of the group and eventually lost sight of the others, who moved faster than he did. Although he was moving slowly, no one from a higher floor ever caught up with him.

"We seemed to be the highest floor where people were able to get out of the building, at least so far as I was able to determine. So there was nobody from above. As we went down, obviously people were filtering in from other floors. We just continued on down in that way," he explained.

As he went lower, water from the sprinklers diminished and then disappeared, which indicated that there were no fires on those lower floors. Later, nearer to the bottom, water appeared again.

Sleigh saw no people running in panic, although many were moving quickly. He said that Port Authority building security officers stationed at several places along the way encouraged people along.

"People walked fairly briskly," said Sleigh. "Every few floors Port Authority people were telling us to hold on to the rails because the stairs were a little wet. They didn't want anyone slipping and hurting themselves on the way down. So we proceeded cautiously but as efficiently as we could."

More than halfway down the building – exactly how far he could not say – Sleigh began to encounter firemen coming up the stairs. The stairs were crowded with people trying to escape and firemen trying to go up. He gave no thought to it at the time, but now he realizes that most, if not all, of those firemen perished.

"On the way down we passed a lot of firemen and rescue workers," Sleigh explained. 'I had experienced this during the '93 bombing. That explosion was down kind of in the center, and affected both towers. The big problem at that time was smoke, a lot of smoke. It forced us to evacuate our floor on that occasion. In '93 we actually just went up on the roof and stayed on the roof until the smoke subsided and we were able to walk down.

"As we were going down the stairway on September 11, firemen were walking up. I felt sorry for those guys, not because I knew their fate but just because of the load they were carrying. They had all the gear with them – 50, 60 pounds of stuff each. Oxygen tanks, axes, and heavy firefighting clothes.

He said it was a struggle for him to go down the stairs. He couldn't imagine how difficult it must be for the firemen to go up the stairs with all their gear. The firemen didn't speak, but he and others tried to offer words of praise and encouragement.

"No, they didn't say anything. We were encouraging them and they were going about doing their job, you know. I guess they were searching floor by floor to make sure everyone was out," Sleigh said.

He never imagined as they passed the firemen that these men were in any unusual danger. Who believed that the entire tower would come down? Even though they were inside the building, their limited perception and lack of information prevented them from knowing how perilous their situation was.

"Only later did the extent of the tragedy sink in – that those guys probably didn't make it out," Sleigh said of the firemen he passed on the stairs. "I mean that was really incredible. A lot of young guys too. Just fresh-faced young guys, 19- or 20-years-old they seemed to be. Yeah, that was disturbing. That thought has haunted me since then. Seeing those people and realizing that they didn't make it."

The trip down from the 91st floor was long and tiring for everyone involved, and it became slower as people from many floors began to reach the bottom, causing a bottleneck.

"As we got near the bottom – and I cannot recall what floors they were – the flow came to a stop a couple of times. With so many people, there was just no movement at all. But there was no panic.

Nobody was shouting 'move along!' Everyone just proceeded down the stairs in a very orderly manner," said Sleigh.

Survivors escaping down the stairs encountered firemen and rescuers coming up the stairs. The stairs were crowded near the bottom of the building, which made it difficult for the firemen to squeeze by. Although few words were spoken, Sleigh said he has vivid memories of the young faces he saw.

"I tell you, the ones who impressed me were the young guys. I just recall seeing a lot of these young guys. One of my colleagues who I was walking down with me said, 'These guys are not even shaving yet.' I mean, that's how young they looked.

"They just looked like young, fresh-faced kids, you know? Those are the ones that I remember. They were stoic as they went about their job, you know. They were serious. They weren't laughing. They weren't wise cracking. They were just going about the seriousness of the job that they were doing. They were going up those stairs not knowing what they were going into, and in retrospect they probably never came out," said Sleigh.

"I was reading some of the accounts recently. I mean, they were told at some point to get out. I mean, there's no point to going any further. And maybe some of them did get out, but I know a lot of them didn't. Look at the numbers of the ones who are missing. It's just incredible.

"Everything is quite vivid in my mind. There was never a point where I lost awareness of what was going on and what was going on around me. I think I have pretty good recall of what I went through," said Sleigh.

During the long climb down, the conversations were few, but when needed Sleigh said he did what he could to reassure those who were struggling.

"I was just encouraging everyone," said Sleigh. "A few women were getting, well, not hysterical but distraught. A little distraught. I just tried to encourage them to keep on walking and kept saying, 'We'll get out.' There was one girl, a Japanese girl walking down with her shoes in her hands. I said, 'You better put those shoes on.' The shoes were not very substantial. I don't know what they would have done when she got outside in all of that rubble. I said you should put your shoes on. You don't want to be walking down without them."

The trip down the stairs was not only emotionally trying for some, it was also a physical challenge and a hazard for many. At places the stairs were wet and very slippery. Sleigh reminded people around him to hold the handrail.

"We didn't want anyone falling down and hurting their back and needing to be carried out. We wanted to make sure everyone walked down and walked out of the building," he said.

Sleigh said he prayed throughout his journey down the stairs. He said his strong Christian faith sustained him and gave him strength. He also prayed for others along the way.

"I have a faith in God that He is Sovereign, and I just prayed. It was his will to spare my life," he explained. "I didn't notice anyone who was praying, but I was praying within my heart. One of the Port Authority people on the stairway directing people, he was very upbeat. He was encouraging every one. He said, 'God has protected you. He'll take care of you.'"

Only 15 minutes after Flight 11 hit Sleigh's building, United Flight 175 sliced through the south tower. Sleigh and the others inside the building who were trying to escape were unaware that this had happened. They still believed the first plane crash was an accident. It never occurred to Sleigh that it was a terrorist attack. He was completely unaware of the attack on the Pentagon, or the crash of United Airlines Flight 93 in Pennsylvania.

"Our group of 11 or 12 had gotten strung out along the way. One other guy was with me most of the way down and then he and I got separated toward the end. We got on to the bottom of the stairwell which is on the mezzanine level of the World Trade Center," said Sleigh.

Port Authority security personnel were at the bottom directing people coming from the stairwells. Sleigh had no way to know if these security people were able to escape.

"They directed us to go one level lower, which is the subterranean concourse level, down an escalator which of course wasn't moving. We walked down, and they directed us through into the concourse," he said.

"The concourse connects all the buildings together. It has a number of stores and various subway stations and the train entrance," he explained.

People were sent to the concourse level to get them away from the building because it was too dangerous to exit the main doors on the mezzanine level. Broken glass and debris were falling from both towers and anyone escaping the building would be at risk of getting hit by that debris. The concourse provided a way for people to get farther away from the towers before exiting into the open.

"Building security people directed us through the concourse and pointed which direction to go. By that time there were 3 or 4 inches of water in the concourse. Sprinklers were going full blast. I was soaked from top to bottom," said Sleigh.

"By now the entire crowd of people who came down the stairwells had sped far enough ahead of Sleigh that he no longer saw them. He and just two other men, unknown to him, were the only ones left. A security guard directed them into a side hallway.

"I just got through the first part of the concourse through one of the side sections or hallways when I heard a huge blast - an explosion. (It came) from the direction of building two (south tower). I still haven't determined what that was, whether it was something that preceded the building coming down, or if it was just an explosion, or if it was the collapse. It was a loud blast. I looked behind me just over my shoulder as I was walking away and saw these sprinkler jets were now going horizontal and huge amounts of debris were flying through the air. So I just started to run away from that as fast as I could," he said.

The blast came from the direction of the south tower. "I was walking out of the north tower and it came from my right which was the direction of the south tower, which is building two. So whatever was happening in building two, whether it was the collapse of the building, or something that preceded it, I don't know," he said.

"I was walking east through the concourse and I was out of its main section that connected building one (north tower) with building two," he added. "I'm not too totally sure where I was. I was a little disoriented at this point. Between the buildings, if you're on the street level, there's a plaza level. I was walking east. I would have been under the plaza level at the point that this explosion occurred.

"And the blast seemed to come from my right and behind me. I was not under either of the towers at the time. I was in the central area that was not directly below the towers."

Sleigh knew that all his co-workers were in front of him, and he had never seen a single person overtake him. He doesn't know what happened to the Port Authority security guards who directed him through the concourse, but when the blast occurred and he looked behind him all he saw was flying debris in the place where the guard had been just moments before.

"Suddenly all the lights went out. It was pitch black. Totally black," said Sleigh. "I stayed on my feet, fortunately. I was just blown by an irresistible force. I had to go with it. It blew me across the concourse.

"I was by myself at that point. I think we were separated, maybe 20 feet apart going through this thing. There was no one immediately around me.

"I was more or less on my own, and I just, I thought that was the end. I really did. I thought that was the end of my life. I just prayed to God to save me, and He answered my prayer. I ended up against a wall of the concourse and a doorway, which seemed to be quite secure. There was this dense cloud of dust that engulfed us, so I just stood there. Thank God for taking me that far. I just waited. It was totally black. I couldn't see a thing.

"And then as the dust settled I started to see some outlines of things. An overhead light was still burning. One overhead light about five or six feet away. I never saw another one in the whole place. I walked over to it and just started to call out, 'Hello. Hello. Anyone around here?' A couple of guys heard me and came over. Together we started to shout out and see if there was anyone there. Some Port Authority security personnel heard us and told us to walk to them. They had flashlights. We just followed their directions to their lights, and they led us out of the building.

"They took us through, and we came up another level of stairs into building five. From there they took us out into the plaza area and then out into the street.

"From the level I came out of building five I saw the concourse area. I did not look back at the buildings. For whatever reason, I didn't do that. I just looked across the concourse area and saw what looked like a war zone. Piles of debris here and there were burning. Horrible things like you might have seen in Beirut. The area was covered with piles of debris."

He emerged exhausted from nearly an hour climbing down 91 stories, soaked to the skin by sprinklers, and covered in soot and dust from debris. It was in his eyes, ears, and mouth. He was disoriented and unaware that his leg had been badly cut by debris that hit him down in the concourse. He had no curiosity to look back at the towers. His whole focus was on continuing to walk away from the disaster he had escaped. Without knowing what happened, he had escaped the worst attack ever on U.S. soil.

George Sleigh is the man with the briefcase on the right in the photo. Photographer Amanda Barbour, was paid for the rights to use this photo.

"I was just covered from head to toe in this stuff. It was incredible. As I was walking out some photographers took some pictures. One of my sons in England called me the next day and said, 'Dad your picture's on the front page of all the London papers here.' I'm the guy carrying the bag," said George Sleigh of his appearance as he emerged from the concourse below the World Trade Center.

"It didn't look like there was a whole lot ahead of me. These two guys I had hooked up with in the building, the three of us were together. We walked out together. I didn't even get their names or anything. We just walked out together, kind of like zombies I guess. There was debris all around and dust everywhere. It was just a mess. Papers. The place was strewn with papers. It was just unbelievable.

"I discovered later that they were taking people out of the building in all different directions. Everybody wasn't coming out of this one exit. By the time we were coming out we were just a few stragglers. I mean, other than the two men I was with I didn't see anyone else left in the building at that point."

Sleigh later learned that his colleagues had been directed out of the building via a different exit, which prevented them from meeting on the outside. Survivors came down many different stairwells and escaped in all directions around the two towers.

Sleigh emerged from the building to a world of total destruction all around him.

"Small fires were burning everywhere," Sleigh said. "I just continued to walk east, away from the complex up Church Street and then up to Broadway. Somewhere along the way I looked down and saw my trousers soaked in blood. I thought I had twisted my knee or something. My knee hurt, and my left ankle hurt, but I just thought it was probably a sprain. So, I just kept walking to Broadway. A police officer there gave me a bottle of water and told me to wash my eyes and my mouth out, which I did. He saw my leg and said, 'You look like you need some attention.'

"An ambulance was there, but it was full, so he walked me north on Broadway for a block and then flagged down an EMT vehicle coming in and put me in the back. They took me to a hospital. As I was getting into that vehicle the cop shouted to the driver, 'Get out of here! The building is coming down!'"

Sleigh said he does not know if the collapse was the south tower, which came down at 9:55 a.m., or the north tower which came down at 10:28 a.m. He did not watch the collapse and did not see the time as he got into the ambulance. He is confused about what happened while he was in the concourse. He doesn't know if the explosion that nearly killed him was in reality the south tower coming down, or if it was something else. If it was the south tower coming down, then he spent an hour coming down the stairs, which he says seems to be longer than what he estimates.

"That's what I was surmising, but I couldn't say for sure. I wasn't looking at my watch to see what time it was. Whether or not the explosion I experienced was the building coming down, I don't think so. It might have been something that preceded the building coming down.

"It sounded like a definite explosion. It wasn't something crumbling and falling. It was an explosion - a bang. Whether the flames had reached a gas main or something I really don't know," Sleigh said.

"It could be (the collapse of the south tower). It could be. I don't really know. I didn't have that understanding at that point. I didn't know precisely what time it was because I didn't look at my watch until I got to the hospital. I was trying to make a phone call to my wife from the hospital and I looked at my watch. It was then 10:30 A.M., so it was a little before 10:30 when I got to the hospital.

"I haven't any other satisfactory explanation as to what that was. It's hardly conceivable to me that it took us an hour to get out of that building, because in '93 when we came down from the roof it took about 50 minutes. And we were coming down maybe 15 floors fewer than in '93, in a well-lit staircase. I just don't really know," said Sleigh, uncertain about much he had experienced.

"When I got into the ambulance the guy gave me some oxygen and checked my leg. There were a couple of deep cuts in my right leg," he said.

"I started to learn what had happened from the ambulance driver. I hadn't known about the second plane hitting the other building or about the attack on the Pentagon. Up until that time I thought one plane had an accident.

"I was just horrified," said Sleigh "But the enormity of what had taken place didn't grab me until later. When I saw what happened I was just amazed that we were able to leave the building.

"The ambulance guy bandaged me up and I got to the hospital. They made me take a shower outside with all my clothes on, just to get the dust off before I went in. I didn't realize how filthy I was. Get all this dust out of me. Out of my face, and out of my nose, and mouth and ears. That kind of stuff. Then they admitted me to the hospital and put me in a cubicle in the emergency section. I took my shoes and socks off and I noticed I had a very deep cut on my left ankle. It was open to the bone and they cleaned it out, squeezed it together, and stapled it shut," Sleigh described.

Sleigh is convinced that no one from a floor higher than his came out of the north tower. He believes he was the last one out from the highest point in the building.

"From the sound of things, and from what I gathered, I have not read any reports of anyone who was above us. If everyone left as promptly as we did they would have all been out and would have come down the stairs behind us," he explained.

The doctor working on him at the hospital had no time because of the number of injured he was dealing with. He said, "I'm sorry we don't have any time today. Hold your breath." He then stapled the wound shut, but Sleigh did not complain. Later he had to return to another doctor for treatment because the wound became badly infected. It had to be reopened, cleaned out, and sewn up. Instead of complaining Sleigh said he was happy his injuries were so minor.

Sleigh was surprised by how few victims were in the hospital that he could see. And he was also surprised at how quickly he was treated and released.

"I was sent to Beth Israel, which is kind of a second tier that would deal with the casualties. There were quite a few people there, but it wasn't overflowing. I mean, they got me right in and got me a cubicle. I didn't have to wait for somebody to leave. I was done and they signed me out by 11:30 that morning," he said.

Sleigh never let go of his big canvas carrying case. He said it may have prevented further injury.

"I caught more grief over that. 'Look at this guy. What a loyal guy. He's still got his briefcase.' I don't know. I just hung on to it. Actually, today, it's a canvas bag, and my wife scrubbed it out and we threw it in the washer and it came out good, but I looked at it today and it's got some cuts in it. Maybe it saved me from some additional debris that may have hit me," he said.

Terrorists twice aimed dead-center, intending in 1993 and 2001 to kill its occupants. Sleigh was in their crosshairs during both attacks, but he was not slain.

Despite the tremendous loss of life, destruction of buildings and businesses, and his own suffering, Sleigh says he doesn't hate the terrorists or those who helped them.

"I'm very angry that they did this," he said. "I don't have any hate in my heart towards them. They're driven by a belief that has been ingrained in them from a false belief system, I believe. They're controlled by people with the power and resources to control and motivate them to do such things. So I have no personal hatred towards them. I don't feel that. I'm just very angry that they would bring so much grief and sadness to so many families.

"I certainly don't think it's over. It was certainly very involved, very well planned, and extremely well-coordinated. So the potential is there for more of the same to happen again," said Sleigh. "I'm just overwhelmed by the evil force that exists in the world."

Sleigh's story is just one of the thousands that could be told about the many escapes from the towers and the buildings around them. Sleigh is unique in that he may have been the last one out from so high up, but he is not unique in that many others had similar experiences. That is why his story is told here, because he helps us to see what it was like for so very many.

Chapter 2

Have you seen my friend Michael?

"What kind of world have we brought our son into?" asked patrolman James Fenn. His wife had just given birth to their first child shortly after he returned from working with rescue crews at Ground Zero.

She snuggled their newborn baby as the 36-year-old father sat close beside them. A television in the background flickered with more news about the attacks. A reporter was talking about possible future terrorism.

"You know, we're heading into the unknown here," he told her. What should have been a moment of joy was instead full of anxiety about the future their son will face. Millions of other Americans now also feel this same ominous shadow of foreboding.

Fenn had been at Ground Zero. The misery of the victims and of those searching for survivors was etched in his thoughts and memories. Images of death and destruction kept entering his mind as he looked at his firstborn child.

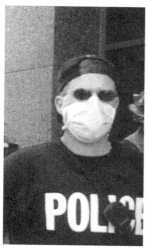

James Fenn

"I don't think I've prayed as much as I've prayed since that night," said Fenn during an interview from his home in New Jersey. "I mean, I've prayed on the way back home on the boat. I prayed before I went to sleep. I prayed the next day. I think I've prayed every day since this has happened. I think this is just the beginning of something we've just never seen before," said the eight-year veteran Rumson, New Jersey, patrolman.

Torn between his desire to be at Ground Zero helping search for survivors and being at his wife's side when his son was born, his emotions ran from one extreme to another. What Fenn had just been through was enough to make even the strongest men sink deep into grief. But he knew he needed to stay strong for his wife and baby son.

"It was a tough situation. We even got into an argument over it," he said. "You know, here you are arguing with a nine-month-pregnant woman. It's like, 'Don't go back,' but you're in a tug-of-war on the inside because you want to go back. I mean, you feel guilt because you want to go back and help."

At Ground Zero Fenn felt like other volunteers who responded to the calls for help on September 11, 2001. Every nearby available police officer and firefighter just stopped what they were doing and went.

"When the first plane hit, I was at home. Then the second plane hit and right after that my pager went off. It said, 'Entire recall for our department.' You didn't really get too long to watch it on TV because they deployed everyone from the surrounding states. Well, I know they blasted out the entire city and state of New York and New Jersey. I think some from Danbury, Connecticut, were helicoptered in.

"However you could get there, you got there. You got there. They sent everyone from Jersey from where I was over on ferries. Helicopters came in from Connecticut. You had the Air National Guard there. And it wasn't as if they waited to be called up. They just came.

"You didn't have to say anything to anybody. Everybody knew they were just going to do what they could do," said Fenn.

Fenn and other police officers from Rumson took the ferry into Manhattan, arriving about 1 p.m. Others from Rumson stayed to guard the ferry against possible attack. The ferry system was needed to bring survivors out of Manhattan and ship first responders in.

"They were worried something was going to happen when they ferried some of the wounded and others back to New Jersey. At the dock the chief assigned me to get one particular military officer to the command center. They were afraid to fly him in, so they took him across on the ferry. This seemed the most secure way to get him there," said Fenn.

"Make sure you get him all the way to the command post," Fenn was told as they departed for Ground Zero.

The original command center quickly proved inadequate. While a new one was being established, Fenn and the officer decided to get a full assessment of the situation by visiting Ground Zero.

This was the scene of total destruction and devastation that confronted them when they arrived.

"We went into the crater as far as we could," Fenn says. "He had been, I guess, in quite a few disasters. But even this veteran paused for a second. He looked at me, because we had talked on the 40-minute ferry ride over. He told me about different things, and when we got there he said, 'Nothing can prepare you for this.' But when he looked at me, I saw that even he was stunned. Then he said, 'All right, we gotta get to work.'

Fenn had heard news reports during those first few hours after the attack. He knew the towers had collapsed. He knew that many of the first groups of police and firefighters had been killed. But he never imagined a scene as horrific as what now filled his eyes.

"The site is huge, overwhelming, I think, for everybody. When you first got there, oh, the bodies! The body parts! It was just awful.

"I had tried to be prepared," says Fenn. "I was trying to set myself up psychologically before we got there because I knew there were going to be a lot of bodies. The number was a lot higher than I anticipated.

"I thought more people had gotten out than did. I had no idea that more than 300 firemen were dead. I guess they lost the whole first and second alarm assignment and then some. Deaths were so high because the night tour rode in with the day tour, so both shifts of these companies arrived to help together.

"I saw a torso. You knew it was a woman because you saw the dress. But in the debris I saw just heads, a leg, a lot of severed arms. I saw a leg with a shoe. It was strange that it was still on the leg. Almost like frozen in time. And lots of bodies were up on the roofs of surrounding buildings, they said. I didn't see any, but reports were coming down," said Fenn.

"We didn't know how devastating it actually was. They located one chief's body when we were at Ground Zero. We found another in line with the Office of Emergency Management."

James Fenn on the left, Sgt. Pat O'Flaherty, and other first responders.

The military officer asked him if any other military liaison was present. He turned out to be the only such person on site. City emergency management officials were busy establishing a new command center and needed a military liaison. They were very close to building 7 of the World Trade Center, which was expected to fall soon.

"The fire department was trying to regroup," Fenn explained. They were going to move the command center to a school because it had land lines. They were having trouble with cell phones. Some worked. Some didn't. They asked the military guy to help them get Humvees. They were calling for personnel transports. They ordered up a whole bunch of helicopters."

It would take time to bring such equipment and National Guard members to Ground Zero, but the wheels were now in motion to make this happen. Requested helicopters never arrived because conditions were too dangerous. The smoke and dust could foul the rotors or engines, and helicopter vibrations would likely cause more debris to fall, potentially killing survivors trapped below.

The men quickly moved off the dangerous street near building 7, which did soon collapse, to what would become the permanent command center to coordinate all activity at Ground Zero.

"I was deployed to a room with what was left of the heads for the city. It turned out to be 'the' command post, not a secondary or satellite one," said Fenn, who was amazed to be so involved in helping set it up.

As soon as radio equipment was operational, the command center was flooded by the sheer number of people trying to talk via radio. The command center was a focal point for communication, and establishing both phone and radio communications with the first responders and rescue workers and the outside agencies whose support they needed was a major task.

"There were so many radio transmissions coming in when we were at the command post. And they were overwhelming numbers…just staggering," said Fenn.

"The military guy I brought there was on the phone with Gov. (George) Pataki or one of his representatives. Anything the city requested had to go through the governor, and he had to have a formal request. Which he did right away. And that started the ball in motion as to getting the military up and going.

"Then they were looking for a current, more detailed assessment, so we had to go back to Ground Zero," said Fenn. He met a group who had just helped doctors set up a make-shift first aid center and morgue. They were watching building 7 because of great concern that it would soon collapse.

Some of the doctors who volunteered to help at the first aid station and morgue.

"We ducked into one of the buildings where the first military specialist on chemical agents showed up. The military guys had a small discussion, then went into a building closed off to everybody else," said Fenn.

Fenn said he saw no evidence of power struggles over which agency would be in charge. Everyone worked cooperatively and helped as needed. Other first responders reported that same harmony.

No turf battles marred team efforts to bring organization out of the chaos that reigns at the start of most disasters.

"Port Authority Police are assigned to certain things down there. They were the first police officers on the scene," said Fenn. "Everyone just went to work. Nobody said, 'You're this,' or 'You're that.' You just go to work. I mean you just start digging. You start on the lines. You start helping guys with stuff. You help them putting stuff on, switching tanks on guys. I mean you just go to work. You dig stuff back. At one point you did crowd control, and at another point you were pulling debris. It was like organized chaos. And everything changed so rapidly."

The years of ongoing training for all police and firefighters paid off, even in the chaos, said Fenn.

"The FDNY, the Fire Department of New York, had their act together totally. The chiefs…they were accountable for their men…were well-organized, sending shifts to key places. When I was there I saw this one chief O'Brien from the fire department. He was extremely together. He was organizing. He had his subordinates taking sections of men and putting them to work. There was accountability, and everyone was…you know…it wasn't a free-for-all," said Fenn.

From the moment he set foot on Manhattan, Fenn was on the lookout for his good friend Michael Chauffey, a firefighter for Engine 54 in New York. At first he just kept looking around wherever he went, but then he started asking other firefighters if they had seen his friend. He knew that Chauffey's company would have been one of the first on the scene, and he was very concerned that Chauffey might be one of the missing.

"They were trying to get logistics together as quickly as possible. The highest ranking official from the Office of Emergency Management was getting over the shock of losing so many good friends and people he worked with. But he was thinking clearly and was extremely organized and good at getting the ball going. The mayor's representative was, like, 'Whatever you guys want. Whatever you guys need.' The police department, same thing. Everyone was on the same page. Then I was cut loose so I could go back to Ground Zero and try to find my friend Michael. He worked for 54 Engine in the city, midtown."

Fenn's digital pager went off. It had a message from his mother that gave him a shudder of dread.

"Your brother's up there. See if you can find him," said his mother's message.

Now he had to find two people he cared for deeply Chauffey and his own brother. He quickly tried to put his own fears aside and went back to work with a prayer in his heart that they would be okay. He joined in with the many others who were removing debris on the main pile at Ground Zero, hoping to find survivors.

"I saw a fireman sitting on the side of Rescue 5 out of Staten Island, and he obviously was upset," said Fenn. "I worked for a fire department before I switched over to the police department. I just looked at him and asked 'How many?'

"He looked up at me. 'I lost them all.'

When the attack occurred, the night shift, or tour, had not yet gone home. The day shift was just starting. Both the night and day shift responded.

Messages like the ones shown on this truck could be found throughout the area written in the dust.

"I guess they lost the whole day tour and the whole night tour. It was right at shift change. Everyone was still there, you know, drinking coffee and whatever when the alarm came in. The city called for a five alarm initially. I guess when the second plane hit they called for another five alarm. Subsequently after that I guess they called for a third five-alarm assignment, so companies were coming from all over," Fenn described.

"On the initial alarm you got all five rescue companies, the building collapse unit, the high rise unit. You got all these specialized units right there," said Fenn. "Their initial command post was right at the base of the towers. So they were trying to organize when you had both towers going. I guess they were in the process of moving it back but they just didn't move it back in time. That's when the first tower came down. It seems to me they were in the talk stages of moving it back. How far I don't know. That's what it seemed to me."

Suddenly what many had expected all day happened. Building 7 was coming down. It made a strange sound as the collapse began, and at first Fenn did not know what it was.

"I looked up, and the first thought that crossed my mind was 'Oh my God! Another plane!' Two other firemen were right by me. We all turned and grabbed each other by the back of the shirt and ran for our lives. Wherever you could grab, everybody grabbed each other and we all just ran as fast as we could to try to take cover. And the building came down and then the cloud...the cloud, you know...I mean it just surrounded you," said Fenn.

When building 7 came down the first responders and rescuers ran for their lives as the debris rushed towards them.

They were less than a block from building 7 and knew they were in a race for their lives. They knew they could never run far enough or fast enough, so they searched urgently to find shelter.

"We got behind one of the fire trucks that was there. It was already crushed from when the towers collapsed. Everyone was just taking shelter wherever they could. Some guys ducked in doorways. Some guys ducked behind buildings. It went straight down. If it's going to go down that's the best way," said Fenn.

When the dust and smoke cleared he was able to get up. Fenn was alive and uninjured. The other men around him were also in good shape. The air was thick with an awful combination of pulverized concrete, smoke from the fire, and a smell that made them feel nauseous. Soon a wind blew in and helped clear the air. His first thoughts were to find his friend and his brother.

"When I went in there, I had black on with my tactical stuff. But after the building came down everything turned gray. You couldn't even see the word "police" on my shirt. I had to get as much of the dust off as I could because you got stopped at certain points if they didn't know who you were. You had to show ID almost everywhere you went."

Fenn was growing more concerned and began approaching firefighters to ask if they had seen Michael Chauffey from 54 Engine. They seemed reluctant to say much and were acting evasive. They knew that 54 Engine had suffered a tremendous tragedy. They did not know about Chauffey, but they had heard that the entire company had been lost when the towers collapsed. Nobody wanted to be the one to tell him.

"When I couldn't find him right away, I started pitching in and dragging stuff out. Then I saw my friend Mike Goshen. He's an iron worker. He came running up behind me with straps for a crane. He saw my P.D. hat from the back with the city of Rumson on it, but he didn't know it was me.

"He said, 'Rumson? What are you doing up here?'

'Mike?'

'Jim?'

"I said," 'Yeah.'

"He said, 'What are you doing up here?'

"I said, 'Everybody's up here. Our chief sent everybody up to Manhattan. We all have different assignments, but Mike, everybody's up here.' And he just kind of looked...because he actually works as an iron worker in Manhattan. You just have that separation. You just think that state lines don't cross sometimes.

"He said, 'Help me carry some of these straps.'

"So I helped him carry some of the straps as far as he needed them to go.

"'You be safe,' he said.

"He's older than me by a few years. He gives me a look like, 'You be safe. Don't get hurt.' Then he climbed up on the crane. They strapped some stuff and tried to drag it back."

Although worried, Fenn knew his brother had come from Newark and would not have been at Ground Zero early enough to be caught when the towers collapsed. His greater concern was for Chauffey because Fenn knew his engine company would have been one of the first to arrive. But he had to put those feelings aside and continue helping where he could.

Abandoned and destroyed vehicles had to be moved to bring in a new wave of first responders and their vehicles.

Heavy equipment was badly needed to begin moving debris. Fortunately, a construction site was not far from Ground Zero. Also fortunately, most heavy equipment starts without a key.

"A couple of the firemen took over the construction equipment....bulldozers and stuff. They just commandeered them. They commandeered anything they could get their hands on to cut some sort of path to get into there," Fenn explained.

Fires were burning in buildings surrounding Ground Zero. Debris continued to fall, making it dangerous for the rescue workers below. The firefighters were using tower ladders to extinguish fires one by one. They also used the long ladders to prevent more debris from falling.

"They were using ladders to prop up some of the stuff. Some of the iron. So much steel, God, so much steel. We were trying to prop things up to make it safe enough just get in to assess what was deeper in the debris," said Fenn.

"So much steel, God, so much steel."

The tragedy took on something painful and personal that Fenn and many other rescuers had never faced before. They came to rescue civilians, but found themselves struggling to find their lifelong buddies, their best friends, their brothers, their fathers, or their own sons. And in that struggle, many found themselves.

Retired police and firefighters dropped what they were doing and came to help. When they heard on the news that over 300 of their former comrades were trapped in the falling debris, they did not wait to be asked to help They grabbed what they had and went.

"The guys who work in the city…they knew so many people…and it turns out that I wound up knowing so many more people than I ever anticipated knowing. Civilians and firefighters," said Fenn of the selfless brotherhood that safeguards civilization.

Exhausted first responders.

Darkness was falling. The day had been physically and emotionally draining for all the rescue workers. They needed to rest but couldn't. They needed food and water, but stopping for such things took precious time that for survivors beneath the rubble could be running out. They wanted to keep searching. Everyone seemed to know someone they could not yet account for. They feared the worst.

"I saw my friend Kevin. I saw the look on his face and he asked, 'Where were you?'

"And I told him what I had been doing. I remember I sat on a bench and he sat me down with me and he said, 'Like, you all right?'

"I was like, 'No, Kevin, I've never seen that, all the destruction and bodies.'

"I was worried because I couldn't find my friend Michael, or my brother. I just started to cry. I said, 'Kevin it was so big of a scene. Everything we did, it just didn't seem like we were putting a dent into anything. It's tough, you know? You train for certain things and you think you kinda can just make all situations better.

"I don't think I'm alone in that feeling. I've talked with lots of people who were there that day, and they said the same things.

They sent so many firemen from down here (New Jersey) and all the police departments from down here sent so many people. Middletown sent up, God, they sent up so many police officers I know," said Fenn of his frustrations and the frustrations of so many others.

"Everyone I've talked to has come back and, just…I mean, you feel that you contributed and you feel that you did the best you could but you just…unless you found somebody alive you just almost feel like you failed. And sometimes it's a little difficult to swallow. I mean you want to find them, and then there's a respect issue so you want to turn them over to New York people and, God, how they must feel about this. You know? The responsibility and everything, because they're the ones that want to find survivors the most. It's their people. You know what I mean? You're over there to help, but it's their people. You totally understand that," he explained.

Fenn said that he and other police and firefighters were talking about their feelings with each other, but perhaps not as much as they should. Those feelings are very difficult to talk about, particularly with people who had not been there in those first few hours. He found it hard to share his feelings even with his wife. Others have told him they faced the same sense of isolation and horror.

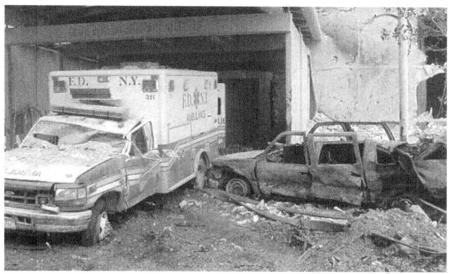

Seeing the destroyed vehicles left by the first responders who perished was difficult.

"It was a little tough. I couldn't talk to my wife about it. She was nine months pregnant. I didn't know who to talk to. You choke on it for a few days, until other guys start to come back. Now I've talked to other people who've been there. Unless you've actually seen it, I don't think anyone can understand. Everybody's asked me, 'What was it like? What was it like?' I'm like, 'I don't know how to put it into words. It was the most devastation I've ever seen or ever want to see. It was a battle zone."

He spoke of the firefighters from Ladder 5 and told how they all died, trapped in a stairwell of one of the buildings. His friend Bobby Davis had recently retired from that very company. These were the men he had worked with, trained, and thought of as brothers.

"They lost eight firemen. Bobby wasn't there. He came into Manhattan. I called him. He told me. From what I understand he was on jury duty. He left jury duty right away, as quick as he could, and then he shot up to Manhattan. And there are so many stories of other guys who are recently retired. They left whatever they were doing and they went. They rushed up to the city, to help their brothers.

"He's retired, but he said all the retired guys came out of the woodwork, went back to their firehouses, grabbed equipment, and went back to work.

"Bobby's a tough man, and for him to even show any emotion, it was…pretty amazing. You can't really talk about it to your wife. You can't really talk about it to most other people. Unless you were there, unless you've been there. You know, he was there in the '93 bombing. He was decorated for some rescues he made in the '93 bombing. He was just…he was so torn, you know. They didn't lose any of his guys then or anything. You know, he was like a senior guy in that firehouse.

"It's killing him. I know it's killing him. I know he just feels some responsibility. I know there were some young kids in the company," said Fenn. Many, many of the rescue workers find themselves dealing with similar feelings and emotions.

"You know firemen. We're always giving each other a hard time all the time. We're always getting on each other, you know. You know police departments. You know, the tough survive. It's not really like that right now. I don't know if it will change back. I'm sure it will eventually. But for right now I guess it's okay for people to just talk about what they've seen, what they're feeling, or whatever," he said very candidly.

Davis also knew Fenn's missing friend Chauffey. He had run into him at St. Vincent's Hospital not far from ground zero, so he was able to tell Fenn that Chauffey had been injured but would be okay.

"Michael was getting his head sewn up a little bit, and they found each other. Because they knew each other before this. I'm friends with both of them and they met each other at my wedding and so they know each other. Bobby found Michael and told him I was looking for him. Michael told him to tell me that he was okay, but I hadn't seen either of them. He went back to work as long as he could," said Fenn of his friend.

Chauffey was not on duty when the alarm came in. 54 Engine responded, but he was not one of those first men who went out. All of them were killed when the towers collapsed. Fenn said it has been extremely hard on Chauffey and the other firefighters from 54 Engine who are still alive. All over Manhattan other engine companies that lost men and the survivors are struggling with the great loss they now feel.

Fenn's friend commandeered a bulldozer from a construction site to clear the way for first responders to get in.

"Michael is a brave son of a bitch. He got up there as fast as he could. He got there and he commandeered one of the bulldozers. He was clearing rubble. He owns a landscaping business on the side. Man, he would not leave. He's so stubborn. They commandeered these bulldozers and some front end loaders and stuff from a job site nearby. They just commandeered them. You know you don't need a key or anything. They just jumped on and crashed through the fences, got them down there, and started clearing stuff away on their own initiative.

"The first night he was operating the equipment. The next day he just dug. They got down pretty far. He was one of the burrowers who went down into one of the holes, and he split his head open pretty bad on a steel I-beam. So he ended up in St. Vincent's and got patched up.

"I guess he went to the firehouse to get cleaned up, get something to eat, take a two hour power nap and then he went back to work. God, he was up there. He didn't even get home until Sunday, and he's got two little babies at home. I kept talking to his wife and letting her know that I kept tabs on him.

"I tell you, man, we took the fire department test together in 1987 in New York. He took the fire department job and I took the police department job where I'm at. We worked together in a Long Branch City fire department in late 80s and early 90s.

"He got where he wanted to be. He always wanted to be in Manhattan. Be in an engine company. You know the pride and everything else that you feel. You know, it overwhelms you. His wife was so worried about him. You know, you worry about his little kids. You know, is he going to be all right? You hear about all the rescue workers that are getting hurt.

"The city that we worked for…Long Branch…they sent up some of the guys that we worked with. A whole bunch of guys came up from Long Branch and they went to work. They were looking for Michael too. I'm sure everybody has some kind of a connection with somebody, or at least a few people, because the numbers are just so large."

Did Fenn find his brother?

"We lost my brother for a couple of days because he works for Newark Fire Department, so he was in Manhattan and couldn't get any kind of contact back to us or from us. It was pretty wild. But he's okay. No problems there. I couldn't find him the first day, but we found him the second day. Yea, it was pretty wild."

Does Fenn expect more terrorism in America?

"I pray to God, 'No!' I hope that Osama bin Laden gave us his best shot and it's over. I hope somehow, some way we can prevent this from ever happening again."

Despite his hope, he acknowledged that police and fire departments have been training for some time in anticipation of an attack using chemical or biological weapons. He said there were teams of specialists checking Ground Zero in case any such weapon was on the planes.

Will fighting terrorism impact our freedoms in America?

"I think some of the freedom of movement we've been used to may be restricted. And you know what? If it makes this a safer place, then I don't have any problem with that. I got nothing to hide, so fine with me. I'm sure there's going to be some concerns, and legitimately so. I haven't really sat down to think about all this, but I'm sure it will be addressed at some level," said Fenn.

Despite the destruction and loss of life, Fenn says he sees some good coming from this tragedy.

"Oh yeah. Everywhere you go around here where I live there's neighbors who don't normally talk to each other who are out talking to each other. People are taking that extra step to talk with each other. Where I live…I can't speak for everywhere…everything I've seen, yeah. People that don't really talk about certain things…I mean emotional things…I mean police, firemen. Let's face it, we just don't talk about emotions. Some of those conversations have come out where I've never seen it before. Especially where I work."

Fenn also said the attack will not cause police or firefighters to quit their jobs.

"I'd say it makes them more determined. I haven't met anybody who said he wants out. I haven't talked to any firemen who said they would leave the job. Most people love the job. I haven't heard of anybody who said they were getting out. Maybe leave and go into the military if that's what it takes, but as far as leaving to get away from danger, no. That's not going to happen," said Fenn with pride and strength in his voice.

Chapter 3

The Cry for Help

Our eyes have seen many pictures of the death and destruction at Ground Zero. But the rescue workers, unlike us, also know this horror through their other senses – especially their sense of smell. Many find it difficult to explain that Ground Zero is permeated with an odor so terrible that they constantly feel like vomiting.

Thousands of dead bodies, ripped to pieces by the collapsing buildings, inevitably began to putrefy. But these were only one ingredient in a devil's brew. To this human carnage were added the dust of pulverized concrete, smoke from many kinds of fires, leaking natural gas with skunk scent added so our noses can detect it, sewer gases, human waste, and a thousand other ingredients from hell's own recipe.

Timothy Hubbard is on the left, in front of one of the main piles at Ground Zero.

This stench filled the noses of rescue workers, no matter what masks they used to prevent it. And like a haunting, the terrible odor followed them home in their clothes and equipment.

"We were in uniform. And my uniform, even though it's been washed, actually still has that smell. When I smell it my mind immediately takes me back," explained patrolman Timothy Hubbard from the Westtown-East Goshen Regional Police Department, 20 miles west of Philadelphia.

Hubbard traveled to Ground Zero with patrolman Bob Balchunis and Cpl. William Cahill from his department. They were deployed to Manhattan in response to a call for help received from the New York Port Authority.

Left photo: Bob Balchunis and Tim Hubbard. Right: William Cahill.

The men had been watching the news throughout the day and responded with enthusiasm to pitch in and help when they were asked to drive to Manhattan. They had recently obtained a special thermal imaging camera that could be used to locate people trapped under debris, and they knew it was important for the search for survivors.

"It was just an unbelievable sight to watch all day on television. It was amazing. You know, the incredible destruction and how things happened," explained Cahill. Later he would say the television images did nothing to show how extensive the destruction really was at Ground Zero.

"Throughout the day we just watched TV, and about 5:30 (p.m.) Sergeant Dwayne Minshall, our operations sergeant, approached me and asked if I'd be interested in leading a team from our department. He asked me and gave me two other officers interested in going up. I was just willing to do whatever we could to help out," explained Cahill.

In addition to having the thermal imaging camera, Cahill is a member of the emergency response team, a SWAT team medic, as well as an instructor at the Pennsylvania Police Academy. They departed for New York at 6 p.m. He graciously provided many of the photos used in this book.

After a fast, but long drive, they reported to a command center at the Meadowlands in New Jersey. They were told that so many volunteers had responded that no more were needed. Cahill and his men knew they had important equipment that may save some lives, so they would not go home that easily.

"We talked to other people and they suggested that we go to one of the tunnels because the Port Authority had actually put out a request. That's how we wound up in New York City," said Cahill.

His determination to find a way to Ground Zero paid off. They reported directly to the Port Authority Police at the Holland Tunnel, and even though they were turning some volunteers away when they learned about the thermal imaging camera they sent the men directly to Ground Zero.

When Cahill and his men arrived they were welcomed with open arms. Travel time and the logistics of finding their way to the right place delayed their arrival at Ground Zero until almost midnight when they were assigned to work directly with a rescue team searching through one of the debris piles.

Cahill's team arrived after nightfall, but even then to see the vast devastation and death at Ground Zero was overwhelming. The men knew it would be bad, but they were shocked by the nightmarish scene.

"Beyond words," described Hubbard. It was just massive destruction everywhere you looked. It looked like a war zone. That's what it looked like. It was organized chaos. The massive amount of debris that was there was just overwhelming. As we were walking up you could see the NYPD guys and the fire department guys trying to do everything they could to save anybody who was in there."

Cahill echoed Hubbard, calling the scene at Ground Zero organized chaos. All the first responders used that term but said that it was a natural thing to expect confusion at the start of any major disaster of this magnitude.

They were all complimentary when describing how well all agencies worked together as the rescue progressed.

Cahill and his crew granted interviews for this book to help the public gain a better understanding of what it was like behind the police barricades cordoning off Ground Zero.

"The pictures on TV don't even begin to reveal what the real destruction is like," said Hubbard. The destruction you see when you're actually there…there's almost no words to describe it. Just the smell alone! And there were still fires, big and small, springing up out of the debris. And the dust and the smell of the smoke.

"You start thinking about all the thousands of people that were in there…people you hoped to find alive. You wonder what it must be like for them because at least I could wear a mask to help me breathe better. As soon as that mask came off that smoke got into your throat and lungs and made you choke. It was so severe that you couldn't even imagine what people stuck in there waiting to be rescued might be going through.

"The smell just kind of brings back into my mind the images of huge pieces of building that hadn't fallen down yet. That's a lot of what I visualize. Debris everywhere. Twisted metal. Concrete and everything. There were walls that hadn't completely fallen down and were several stories high. And buildings that still had some stories left to them. It was actually like a lower level of the World Trade Center," said Hubbard.

Despite all the sights, sounds, terrible smell, and the risk of more debris coming down on them, Cahill and his men got ready to put their equipment to work. They had high hopes that they would find some survivors. They tried to focus only on the job at hand so that they could avoid being distractions, remain alert – and maybe find someone under the wreckage still alive.

Destruction and chaos were beyond anything they had trained for.

"Sure, I saw body parts, but I think because it was parts and they weren't anything substantial, or identifiable as a particular person, I think you could kind of disassociate yourself," explained Hubbard. "At that point I was much more focused on the life to be saved than the death all around me."

"They went to work on one of the main piles and started to use the thermal imaging camera, expecting it to help them find warm, living bodies they could save. This technology gives humans a new sense, the ability to "see" heat. In nature the Sidewinder and other rattlesnakes uses such a thermal sense to zero in on warm-blooded prey. So does its namesake, the heat-seeking air-to-air Sidewinder missile.

"It's a thermal imaging unit that we recently received from the Federal Government through their counter-drug program. It looks like a camcorder. It's a handheld device similar to infrared. It's a thermal image. It picks up heat sources," explained Cahill.

The men used the camera to scan extensively through the debris. The sophisticated device could see through quite a few feet of debris, so they tried to cover as much area as possible. Soon they realized they had a major problem using the camera.

"For the first hour we used the camera, but it didn't seem that it was really aiding us. We weren't coming up with anything because everything was pretty hot at that point. The debris was extremely hot, so after the first hour we actually locked the camera up. From then on our search was basically just hands and knees. Just digging and moving and handing out pieces of debris. And once in a while we were a human line handing equipment in and bringing debris out," said Cahill.

The debris in the pile was so hot the thermal camera was ineffective.

Although disappointing, the problem was easy to understand. The camera was sensitive to heat, and the debris itself was hot because of all the fire that had been in the towers. The debris was hotter than a trapped person would be. Human body heat, like white camouflage in a field of snow, could not be detected amid debris that was the same temperature – or was hotter.

"Everything was still very hot. I noticed when I was using the viewfinder that I wasn't finding anything. It then just made more sense to move things piece by piece by hand and visually search without the thermal imaging," Cahill explained.

And so they put the camera aside, got down on their hands and knees, and dug through the night and into the next day. It was physically and emotionally demanding, yet they kept going without complaint. The search was challenging. Everyone wanted so much to find survivors, but the more they searched the more death they found. And the more exhausted they became.

"I think you got so caught up in the job you were doing and concerned for the people you were trying to help that weariness didn't set in unless you stopped. You were able to push it aside almost, but once you stopped, once you said we need to take a step back and sit down, as soon as you sat down to rest for a moment everything rushed right over you and you were completely exhausted mentally and physically," explained Hubbard of the tremendous strain they were all experiencing.

Police and firefighters must participate in extensive ongoing training to hone and improve their skills in many areas. Many hundreds of hours are spent improving their ability to deal with every imaginable challenge. Cahill brought his cameras because he participates in such training. He also teaches at the police academy and wanted to use the photos for future training. Many of those photographs were generously provided by Cahill for use in this book.

"I took those photographs during each break primarily to use in training. I'm an instructor at the police academy, and I was hoping to use some of that," said Cahill. Although he said the planning he has had in the past was very helpful to him, it was virtually impossible to be ready for such devastation.

"I'll be honest with you. You can do all the pre-planning in the world, but there's no pre-planning that will prepare you for something like this. Complete devastation. It's unbelievable, even when I think back," he added.

The rescue workers are trained in ways to help people in danger, but they are also trained to avoid injury themselves. They cannot help anyone if they, too, become victims.

Tired and discouraged first responders.

"We were all determined to do what we could for the victims. Then, also, we wanted to make sure each of us was okay. We'd see somebody in the line ready collapse, so we'd talk to them and next thing you know they'd take a little break. They needed a break but they were so overworked, so overwhelmed with everything. There were some guys that had just gotten to a point where they were collapsing," Cahill said.

The teamwork and united effort by all agencies was a significant factor in the early rescue efforts.

"I think we were as well prepared as anybody could be, yes. I think because it was such a massive, massive scene. Even so, as big as it was the efforts put forth by everybody there, you just kind of knew where to fit in. Everybody knew what they needed to do. If somebody saw a hole that needed to be filled to do this job or that job, somebody would step up and fill in," said Hubbard.

They all said that everyone worked well together without any struggles for power or authority. No egos, and no turf battles.

"Not in the least," said Hubbard. "Other times, putting this situation aside, you hear of things like that between fire and police and what not, but everybody was just working one right along with the other. If a NYPD guy said we needed a tank of oxygen over here for the rescue workers, someone would just bring it. It was a very unified effort by everybody."

The long night was filled with frustration and with emotional and physical strain. But morning light brought with it the hope of a new day. As sunlight filtered through the smoke and dust, Cahill and his men found new energy and hope with the announcement that a survivor was about to be pulled from the debris. Rescuers formed a life line, a type of bucket brigade to pass debris from one man to another to clear a path through the debris to the policeman found alive buried in the rubble. They had been working the line all night, and now their efforts were about to pay off.

Cahill, Hubbard, and Balchunis felt their tired bodies fully awaken. The long night's effort was producing at least one example of the success they and all the other rescuers so desperately needed to boost their morale. All three men joined the long line of rescuers who carefully helped pass debris from the area where the rescue was taking place across the pile and out of the way.

Work had continued all night. Rescuers found the survivor by tapping on the debris pile and hearing his response. The digging began in earnest. They soon reached the police officer, but his lower body was badly trapped. A doctor came in to treat him. Teams of men worked carefully through the night to free him from dangerous debris that might suddenly collapse and kill them all.

"He was in there through the night. They would pass in IV bags, and I know there were doctors going in and out of the line attending to him, changing IV bags, things like that. This went on for hours. I never saw him during that time, but from what I understand, he was trapped from at least his waist down - his lower extremities," explained Hubbard.

This police officer's rescue was the most memorable part of his trip to Ground Zero, Cahill and Hubbard agreed. The rescue provided a tremendous boost to the rescue workers who had worked so hard, many since the first plane had hit 24 hours before. The amount of debris and precarious way it was tangled around the survivor created a risky challenge for the rescuers to overcome. There was no room for error.

"I wasn't working where the police officer was, but I could see him while he was being dug out," explained Cahill. "He was farther in than where I was located. Their number one concern was his medical condition. They couldn't see what the bottom half of him looked like, so they didn't know if he had any injuries. Volunteer doctors had actually gone all the way into the hole where he was and were doing what they could. I know they had a hard time getting an IV into him.

"I think it was just overcoming the amount of debris and the way it was just twisted. He was just so stuck in there. Little by little they chipped debris away from him until they could say, 'Okay, it's safe to get him out without injuring him or anyone else.'"

Cahill and his men were working together, side by side, passing debris as it came from the rescue site. It was a long line that was formed to get the debris out of a very dangerous location.

"He was probably some 200 to 300 yards in from the street in the midst of the debris. To get him out, a human chain formed to pass him out from that debris to the waiting medical team. But the neatest part was that as he was getting passed outward he was looking up at people and saying, 'Thank you, guys. Thank you so much,'" said Hubbard.

The survivor was actually strapped into a basket-type stretcher and had to reach up and take his oxygen mask off in order to talk to them. As he passed in front of Cahill's men, the rescued officer took his mask off and thanked them.

"That will stay with me more than anything else," said Cahill of the experience.

"It's something I'll never forget," commented Hubbard.

There was a loud cheer and lots of applause as the officer came out and was loaded into a waiting ambulance. Groups of workers throughout the area, too far away to even see what was happening, heard the cheers and joined in. They knew that the only thing that could generate this kind of response after a long night was a successful rescue.

Cahill said he believes this was the last, or next to the last, survivor to be found alive. But he and his men never did hear the name of the officer. They knew only that a brother officer had been trapped and needed help. That's all they needed to know.

The rescuers felt a renewed life and energy. Inspired and uplifted, they went back to work on the several piles of debris seeking more signs of survivors. But the debris was still too hot, and the thermal imaging camera still would not work.

"Everything was just twisted metal everywhere covered with the dust, and then things were hot," explained Cahill. There were I-beams that were extremely hot. Small fires around us constantly kept re-igniting. Most of the metal we were on was wet. That caused all kinds of hazards. When they brought in heavy equipment, the pile started shifting. That was a pretty scary deal for us.

Construction workers volunteered to help move debris.

"They brought in heavy equipment, actually front-end loaders, and moved the debris we were piling up. When they pushed that debris, the ground would move and shake from vibrations. Debris would fall from the buildings that were still standing. It was unbelievable."

The use of the heavy equipment brought concern. The vibrations and pressure it created could cause the piles to shift and collapse further, endangering rescuers and anyone caught in pockets below. For that reason these machines worked only on the outer edges of the debris.

"Yea, at one point on Wednesday morning they started to bring in some heavy equipment to move some debris along the outer edges," said Hubbard. "Every so often you would feel the vibrations, and I don't think it was the vibrations of the buildings getting ready to fall. I think it was vibrations the heavy equipment was sending through the debris. You know, they made you pause for a minute and look back and make sure the buildings around you were still doing what they were supposed to."

The team from Pennsylvania was now exhausted. It was time to leave. Theirs was an experience none wanted ever to repeat, but they also said that some good came of it.

"It was difficult, but until we left it (emotion) really didn't hit me," said Cahill about his personal feelings as he reflected on his experience. It was such a devastating thing. And to see the grief on the New York City cops and the New York City firemen. The grief on their faces. Their determination gave us determination to continue. It was amazing.

It was beyond anything they had trained for or expected, but they all managed to find a way to overcome the challenges.

"We were working with cops in an environment we never worked in before. But we were all on the same team and everybody knew what needed to be done. We didn't have to communicate when we were going to grab something, or move something, or attempt to move up on another section of debris. It was unbelievable how the teamwork happened. Everybody was just so focused that we just worked together to find more survivors. That was what we were real determined to do."

At times, even big, tough policemen had to take some time to just let it all out. Fortunately they were able to help one another other deal with those moments, regain strength, and move on.

"I actually experienced that myself," said Cahill. "I actually cried with another guy. It was just unbelievable. And one thing that was nice is that we have a chaplain with our department and he was there to greet us when we got back. That made our return much easier. That was a real positive thing for us when we got back to talk to him."

Hubbard said the only thing he had to give him strength to deal with it all was his faith in God.

"I think the biggest thing that helped me through both the physical and emotional strain was just knowing that by just taking a minute, and even though I'm still working, praying. And asking that I can have that extra effort and that extra strength that I need to get the job done," explained Hubbard.

He said he was not the only one who prayed.

"You'd see firemen and policemen, mostly from the New York City units. Basically they'd just be down – whether they were resting or not I can't say – they'd be down on one knee just kind of having their head bowed and their eyes closed. Certainly it appeared that they could have been taking a moment and just talking with God and asking for His hand to help hold them up.

"I was raised in a Christian home. Ever since I can remember I have always been somebody who…you know I went to a Christian high school…and it's always been something I've been very focused on in my life. My faith has always been very, very important to me in everything, in all aspects of my life," explained Hubbard.

Both Hubbard and Cahill said they fully expect more terrorist attacks on America, and the challenge for everyone in the country will be great.

In light of his strong Christian faith, what does Hubbard think about the terrorists who did this?

"You begin to think about that, and after a while you almost feel sorry for them. Their life is so focused on something that's so wrong and so inhumane. Their focus is to destroy Christianity and innocent humans. I actually started to feel sorry that they had to live like that. Over the long-term, I think it's going to be a situation for America and the world that no one has been exposed to yet in terms of battling people who feel that way."

The actions of those terrorists brought death and destruction to innocent people. Lives were destroyed, families will be forever damaged, and life in the U.S. will never be the same. Firefighters and police officers rushed into a burning building to save the lives of others. Many asked for and receive the last rites of the Catholic Church before going in.

Did the firefighters and police know that they were putting themselves in grave danger in an effort to save lives?

"Absolutely," said Cahill. They did it for their country. There's no doubt about it. It's a direct result of what those good people did that they lost their lives. They actually gave their lives for others."

What would you say to their children?

"I would want them to know that their father or mother was an absolute hero of our country," said Cahill. "No doubt about it. Those people went in there knowing the risks. They took those risks to save lives. And as a result they saved many, many lives. They're absolute heroes. They should be remembered forever.

"That whole experience has changed me forever. I'll never forget helping to carry out that officer. I'll never forget all those grieving people. I think it's made me a better person."

Chapter 4

Organized Chaos

Pat O'Flaherty grew up on the streets of Dublin, Ireland. Like many an Irish youth he dreamed of seeking his fortune in America. Ireland's greatest export has been its people, the saying goes, and O'Flaherty became one of its finest.

Americans of Irish descent make up about 40 percent of the police and fire forces in New York City (the traditional Irish professions) according to the Irish Voice. A large number of undocumented Irish also work in New York, particularly in the construction trades. Many construction workers were lost from the attacks when the towers fell. News reports estimate that at least 30 who died were undocumented Irish natives.

"The Irish feel a very deep affinity to this because a lot of those police and firefighters were Irish. My heart goes out," said O'Flaherty.

Like so many others, O'Flaherty first learned of the attack on the World Trade Center as he watched the morning news on television. When the immensity of the loss became obvious after the collapse of the towers, he knew he had to do something to help. He is now a sergeant in the New Jersey National Guard and has served for many years, including a tour of duty during Desert Storm.

"I was wrestling with my conscience because I wasn't on orders," O'Flaherty explained. Even though there was no call-up as yet, he decided to jump into his uniform and see what he could do to help. Sgt. O'Flaherty headed for the ferry with the hope he could get to Manhattan.

"I frankly am a little concerned that they may try and bust me down in rank. I don't know if they will or not. I felt that I had to get over there, and I felt it was more important that I was in uniform because people respond better in emergencies, and it really did work well," explained O'Flaherty.

First he spent some time helping survivors who were coming out of Manhattan on the C Street Ferry.

"As I saw them coming off shell-shocked, suffering from smoke inhalation, all covered in dust. I was wrestling with my conscience. I knew I needed to help on the other end," said O'Flaherty.

He decided he should do a lot more than help survivors get off the ferry. He wanted to go where he could be of more help, so he joined other police and firefighters getting on the ferry to go over as volunteers.

"We came in by boat to pier 11 on the east side of Manhattan, which is just south of the Seaport Ferry. The smoke was blowing, and it was bad. People were running off the boat with masks on. I had no mask because I'd given mine to someone else earlier on," he explained.

A passenger getting off gave him a mask and said, "You're going to need this."

He arrived in Manhattan, asked how he could help, and was sent directly to Ground Zero with a police escort to get him there quickly.

James Fenn and Pat O'Flaherty at Ground Zero.

"It was still chaos when I got there. It was still pretty bad. You know, the ashes were still flying around bad. You could hardly breathe," he described. But shortly after he arrived he and the other rescue workers had to leave.

"The building in front of us was actually groaning, so we moved back," he said.

What he saw was a "thousand times worse" than anything he saw during Desert Storm.

"I was in the desert at the end of Desert Storm. I saw a lot of damage and destruction, but this was worse. The sky was dark. The ash was thick. You were coughing your lungs up with the dust. Everything was covered in two inches of this dust, this asbestos hazardous dust, which we were all breathing in.

"Everything was gray and full of paper."

"The whole place was gray. Everything was gray and full of paper. It was bizarre. Like the aftermath of a ticker tape parade. If you looked at the papers you saw bonds and checks and personal checks. I picked up a piece of paper to look at. It had World Trade Center Port Authority on there. It was a drawing of one part of one of the buildings they were working on or something," O'Flaherty said.

He was working with several others as they tried to find a way around the groaning building to get to Ground Zero. As they moved carefully around and through the debris fields, they ran into some aircraft parts. The largest identifiable piece they found was a landing wheel, still completely intact.

"Moving forward again, we started to see human remains, body parts and half bodies and the like. Just lumps of muscle, tissue, you know. There was half a body that had been diagonally sliced from across the breast down to the crotch with a piece of a leg. We used cones to cover those up, because we had nothing else to use at that time," he said.

After looking at the confusion, and through discussions with representatives from fire and police units, O'Flaherty realized that he and Mike Moore were the only military representatives there at that time. Moore is a power rescue technician in the New York Air National Guard rescue unit. He, too, showed up on his own initiative.

"There's only 300 of them in the world. They're specialized rescue technicians. They go down and rescue pilots who have been shot down behind enemy lines. In my previous experience I worked 11 years for what they call a Long Range Surveillance Unit. It's a reconnaissance patrol unit. You work in six-man teams. You're all airborne-qualified. You're highly specialized. And you go behind enemy lines to create havoc or create intel," O'Flaherty explained.

Both towers had already fallen by the time O'Flaherty arrived on the scene. His military training and experience had taught him how to look around, evaluate the situation, consider available resources and needed resources, and consider how he could best help the situation. He saw that the rescuers needed organization at Ground Zero. He was grateful he found Moore. The two already knew each other and were ready to go to work.

They decided that they should move as close to the center of the destruction as possible. An assessment was needed, and a command center was essential to coordinate the work of different organizations and find resources needed. A command center is a focal point of communication that helps change a haphazard effort into an organized one.

"Now, bear in mind, although we were in uniform, we don't work for the city. It was chaos. Everybody was running around in a daze. We were just trying to help where we saw a need. When we got there, it seemed like the guys who were responding were all in shock," O'Flaherty explained.

"My first urgent task was not looking for survivors myself," he went on. "Plenty of people standing around dazed were ready to do that as soon as they got organized. My objective was to start getting this equipment they needed, and the people they needed, and the infrastructure needed to so that all these rescue workers could start looking for survivors. That was my objective."

Plenty of human resources were available, but no centralized organization was yet directing and coordinating the search effort. Rescue workers had no means to communicate a need for help, coordinate the work of different groups, or request special equipment.

There were plenty of human resources, but they were waiting for direction.

"No infrastructure was in place to start bringing all these assets together. Not just equipment but dogs, people, food, and whatever else it took.

"My friend and I raced up town a couple blocks, and we found a police officer from OEM (Office of Emergency Management) of some sort. I forget his name. What a miracle. He barely got out of the garage in one of the World Trade Center buildings. It was collapsing around him as he got out," he said.

The OEM officer regarded O'Flaherty and Moore as military liaisons, and they all began to work together. In the first few hours the command center was a mobile bus, but that quickly proved inadequate. They began a search for a nearby building to house the people and equipment needed facilitate communications.

"We found a school where we started setting up. We were the first military guys in that facility to set up a military liaison operations center. All these military people were showing up in uniform on their own, just volunteering. I set up a system whereby we could use them. We used a school that had a theater where we could work," said O'Flaherty.

With the command center up and running, it was now possible to organize work crews and dispatch them to areas with specific assignments. Chaos was becoming organized.

"Then as we started to get organized and get requests for help, I dispatched these guys in teams to go and help, escort, bring food, whatever. We worked together to come up with ideas to get things done more effectively," said O'Flaherty.

The actual transition from chaos to "organized chaos" took place gradually throughout the afternoon and evening. But even with the existence of a physical location for the command center, the biggest difficulty was communication.

"We just started getting a grip on things, and I would run down to the zone myself. I would find these firefighters who do the rescue work. I would physically grab one and say, 'Hey listen. I'm working up here for the liaison with the military. What do you need? What are you lacking? What can I do? What can I get you right now that will get you back to work searching?'

"And they would start passing these requests, and I'd run back up to the command center because we didn't have any communications yet. I passed the word, and Mike started working on the rescue dogs.

"It was chaos for about 6 hours, then it turned to organized chaos. I mean really, it was. It turned to organized chaos when the various agencies started meeting together. They began getting all these different groups to organize, getting the right equipment, and what was necessary to run a good rescue mission."

They could hear a "groaning" sound from building 7.

When O'Flaherty first arrived, he had difficulty getting to Ground Zero because the area around building 7 was closed off. Actual "groaning" sounds came from the building, and it was burning out of control on virtually every floor. Firefighters warned that it would soon come down, but when it did some were still caught by surprise.

"When that building collapsed, about 800 people ran. When you see firefighters running like hell and jumping through plate glass windows, you know you've got a problem," said O'Flaherty. It was like something out of a movie. The building started to collapse downwards, which was not bad, but then it started coming right towards us. I'm not sure, but I think that building was about 60 stories. So we knew from the destruction of the other buildings that we were in trouble. I started running like a maniac."

The sound of the collapse was like a roaring freight train, growing ever louder as it came closer. The dust and smoke did not just billow up as a fluffy cloud. It had the appearance of a solid wall, and large chunks of debris could be seen flying in and around it. It was ominous and horribly frightening.

The collapse of the building seen from several blocks away.

"I remember looking behind me one time, and I saw this thing coming towards me, like in a movie, and I remember saying, 'Jeeze! I just got here and I'm going to die. I can't believe this. That stinks!' I actually did say that. But as we got towards the end of the block it stopped. The whole building seemed to be coming at me. The dust was so thick that you couldn't tell if it was just dust or was the whole building coming at you," said O'Flaherty.

He said everyone looked around in amazement at what had happened. Some were overcome by the dust from the collapse and smoke from the fire. A wind came in and helped clear the air. Once the collapse stopped many who ran to safety tried to run back to check the debris for anyone who might have been trapped. Police and others stopped them because it was too dangerous.

"Police were holding them physically back. Then finally they got permission to go back in. They organized and went in to see what they could find," but he was unaware of anyone who needed to be rescued because of this collapse.

The rescue effort continued into the night. Body parts and pieces were collected and sent to a makeshift morgue. It was a grisly task that demoralized the workers.

"They brought these human remnants to the aid station. Eventually they'll try and identify the body parts through DNA, I guess. What a horrible task," remarked O'Flaherty.

The rescue workers came with the hope and expectation of finding people alive in the rubble. Instead they found pieces of what were once their friends, neighbors, and even family. The anonymous pieces were once mothers, fathers – people just like themselves. A pall of depression and hopelessness crept over the hundreds of rescuers spread throughout Ground Zero as darkness settled in. The work continued, but it was almost impossible to remain hopeful when death hung in the air and lay in pieces on the ground all around them.

"If they could find just one person, then this would give them some hope again," explained O'Flaherty. A group of rescuers gathered to discuss possible places they might find survivors.

If we could find a way to get to the underground mall area, we might find someone alive. That guy who escaped the parking garage, well, that's one level below the mall area. So, maybe there's a possibility," he said. Suddenly there was reason for hope, and a group was organized to search for a way into the area to determine if anyone could be found alive.

O'Flaherty continued to meet with first responders and figure out ways to organize the search effort so that it could evolve from random, hit-or-miss search efforts to ones that might find someone alive.

The coordination effort was difficult because communications were difficult. Often the easiest and fastest way to convey information was to send human messengers. That task was arduous because of the distances involved and the physical obstacles and dangers in the way.

"There's not just one pile they're working on. There's like six different piles. It's not one little area," explained O'Flaherty. He said television makes it look like one pile in one central area, but in reality there are multiple piles of debris as well as craters. The piles were also very unstable and tended to actually move and shift when workers tried to walk on the rubble.

One of the many "piles" at Ground Zero.

"Lots of retired and off-duty guys just showed up. No one told them to come, you know. They just knew and they showed up. It was like that," he explained.

O'Flaherty met up with others such as Cpl. William Cahill and his crew from Pennsylvania, who told of his frustration because his thermal imaging camera was ineffective. He also spent time with patrolman James Fenn from New Jersey. Together, they and others ran for their lives as the building came down.

In the morning, when Cahill's group was helping with the rescue of the police officer, a large cheer went up that could be heard for blocks. Others heard the cheers and joined in because it was a welcome sign of success.

"I was a block north of it. You could hear them cheering, though. Oh yeah, you could hear them cheering. You could tell they got him out. It was great. Everyone stopped and joined in the cheers," said O'Flaherty.

Although he has had all types of disaster training, nothing prepared him for the effects of the attack on the World Trade Center. The closest preparation he knew of was a disaster simulation run by Con Edison, the electric company, in which a small light plane accidentally flew into a high-voltage tower.

"Who could have thought that not one but two fully fueled commercial aircraft would hit both buildings?" asked O'Flaherty.

Now he says that plans must be made for the next attack, which he believes is inevitable.

"I think we have to think of the worst possible situation imaginable and plan around that," he said.

The entire experience has been extremely emotional for him. It has brought him back to church after a long absence.

"I went and got a blessing from the priest, and I took the host. I haven't taken the host in years. It was very emotional for me," O'Flaherty said. He added that the death of Catholic priest Mychal Judge, who died while administering to rescue workers, touched him deeply.

He said there were men who were devastated emotionally by the loss of people they knew, and also by the sights they encountered at Ground Zero.

"They're going to be haunted with these things for life," he added.

For O'Flaherty the greatest heartbreak has come as he has faced grieving family members who came into the area combing through the rubble, desperately searching for a lost loved one. They carried pictures of their family member and pleaded with him, tears streaming down their cheeks, "Please help me." They were just wandering the area, not really knowing what to do. Crushed by their loss.

"It's very heartbreaking. Sometimes I go off by myself for a while to deal with it, you know," said O'Flaherty.

This book covers the first hours after the attack, but it is important to note that O'Flaherty came home only to sleep and continued to work at Ground Zero day after day.

Chapter 5

Mass Exodus

"It's coming down! It's coming down! Oh my God, run!"

Screams filled the air outside the south tower of the World Trade Center at 9:55 A.M. the morning of September 11, 2001, less than an hour after United Airlines flight 175 crashed into it.

People who had escaped from the towers, including police, firefighters, and other rescue workers, were running for their lives. Some took shelter inside, beside, or beneath fire and police vehicles that littered the streets around the tower. Most of those vehicles would be crushed by falling debris, and many also caught fire and were incinerated.

Debris from the towers damaged and destroyed other buildings.

Hundreds of first responders and thousands of civilians were trapped inside the tower when it came down, and more were buried alive by the debris. As the tower literally disintegrated and collapsed upon itself, massive chunks of concrete and steel rained death on the people in the streets below.

DAVID M. BRESNAHAN

The debris also damaged other buildings. The north tower was badly damaged at its base by falling debris, and fires ignited in its bottom floors from flaming rubble and gas explosions. Building 7, the American Express Building, also suffered structural damage and flames rapidly spread from its top to bottom.

Other buildings throughout the complex were heavily damaged and also began burning. The blazes were too extensive for firefighters to control or extinguish. They turned their efforts to bringing people to safety. They knew the intense heat from the fires would soon soften the beams and bring the north tower and building 7 down as well.

Lt. Maurice Ottolia, 46, of Brooklyn North Narcotics stood at the intersection of West Street and Liberty, unable to believe that what his eyes beheld was real.

Lt. Maurice Ottolia.

"It was like "Apocalypse Now" and 'Dante's Inferno" and a few other such things all wrapped into one," said Ottolia.

That morning Ottolia was getting ready for work and was flipping through the channels on his television when he saw a picture of the World Trade Center with one of the towers burning. He didn't think it was real, but he was curious so he stopped and watched for a moment.

"I'm thinking it's some kind of, you know, video game or they're reviewing some film for special effects," explained Ottolia.

Nowadays video games and Hollywood magic have made it almost impossible to separate reality from fantasy.

"And then I realize it's a live news feed. At that point I knew they're going to be mobilizing a lot of police officers and firemen. It hadn't collapsed yet, but as soon as it collapsed I knew for sure that we'd all get mobilized," he said.

He rushed to work, but as a detective he was unsure about whether he would be deployed to the World Trade Center. It wasn't until he arrived and word came of the collapse of tower one that he began to understand how devastating the attack was.

"As soon as I got into work the whole building was mobilized. I happen to work in Brooklyn North Narcotics. Usually we don't get mobilized for things like that. Usually we're kind of on our own. Usually patrol services are the ones who go out first. In this case it was an 'all hands' kind of thing. Everybody had to report down to West Street. As we got down there they started moving people out right away, mostly to the area of the collapse," he said.

"They couldn't fight the fire in the tower because they couldn't get close enough."

It was unlike anything he had ever seen or experienced. Books and papers were lying on the ground and blowing in the air for at least three blocks all around Ground Zero. Dust covered everything. The air was full of thick smoke, and the smell was intense. The north tower was burning intensely, up at the top where the plane hit but now at the bottom too. And other buildings were also burning and damaged by debris.

"I just feel terrible for the firemen and police who were killed. I knew some of them personally. My father-in-law's been a fireman for 32 years. He retired some time ago. So we understand the feeling. It's indescribable really. It's never happened in the history of New York. Nothing this big in the way of firemen and police killed on the job," said Ottolia.

The firefighters and police who survived after the collapse of the south tower wanted to rush in and do what they could to rescue more people. But it was far too dangerous. They had to hold back or they would all be killed.

"At that time the place was still in flames. To say it was indescribable is redundant. The word has been overused, but that's the best word to describe it - indescribable. As you walked up West Street you were seeing books and papers a far as two or three blocks away. At that time number 7 World Trade Center hadn't collapsed yet. That was still standing. They were talking about it and said we can't get too close to that. We can't fight any of the fires.

"It seemed like they couldn't fight the fire in the tower because they couldn't get close enough. We knew it was going to collapse because it was out of control. The bottom floors were gone. The top floors were in flames. The bottom floors were gone because of the debris from the collapse. The lower floors weren't intact. It was right next to number one," described Ottolia.

There was no way in, and for many there was no way out. It was a desperate situation and there was nothing the first responders could do but withdraw a safe distance, watch, and wait. They looked in horror as one person after another jumped to their death from the higher floors of the tower. With fire all around them and no way to escape, dozens chose to jump rather than burn. Some were also blown out of the building as explosions threw people and debris to the streets below.

The best that first responders could do was evacuate nearby buildings. They rushed into neighboring buildings to warn people to leave before there was another collapse. Very little could be done in the way of rescue attempts until both towers and building 7 were down and the dust and debris had settled. Building 7 came down at 5:20 P.M., so it was evening before crews were able to move into Ground Zero, according to Ottolia.

"We couldn't really attempt any rescue efforts. Some people kept trying to get close on the fringe and do 'search and rescue' in adjoining buildings to see if there was anybody, alive or dead. But as for Ground Zero, nobody was really getting into that area. It wasn't until nightfall that they started moving the debris on West Street to try to get closer. I think the pedestrian walkway bridge number one or north collapsed on top of a fire engine, vans, and ambulances. It was unbelievable.," he said.

A pedestrian walkway bridge collapsed on top of vehicles.

"An Emergency Services police officer told me they had lost at least 14 or 15 of their own. I said, I know we lost some firemen, but we also lost some police officers."

"He said, 'Yeah. I was standing here when it came down. I know where they are. I know exactly where they are, but we can't get to them.'

"That's how close they were. He saw it come down. He knew where they were, but they couldn't get to them until the latter part of the week."

Smoke rising from the collapsed building.

"At that point it was basically a waiting game, because when it did collapse I was speaking to an out-of-state police officer with a medic. We were speaking, and even before we had the chance to take any photos, we were all talking about how that was going to come down soon. They were all predicting that it would come down. As we were talking, low and behold, it came down," Ottolia described.

In other areas around Ground Zero rescue workers dodged falling debris and fires, desperately trying to find anyone alive they could save. Their efforts were in vain, and some rescue workers were getting hurt. Many were cut by falling glass and debris. Several rescue workers said they heard stories of firemen who were killed.

As soon as the rescuers would make some progress moving debris they would be called out of the area for safety concerns. When they would finally have an opportunity to go back they found the work they had done was now covered by new debris and they had to start over again. The real meaningful digging through debris was not able to begin until evening.

"When we finally did begin to dig, within the first hour of when we started looking for survivors, we found two people – just basically bodies. We had no idea what they were. They were just under the debris on West Street there. I think some rescuers found a fire officer not too long after that – killed in the collapse," said Ottolia.

He spoke of the frustrations of the rescue workers who desperately wanted to find survivors. They couldn't get in close enough to search, and when they did get in they were soon called back because of falling debris. When at last they began a full search, in their hearts they knew that the destruction had been so violent that finding survivors was unlikely. Everyone kept hope. No one wanted to admit what they really knew deep inside – that thousands were dead and almost nobody had survived to be rescued.

Other frustrations existed as well. Many police were unable to go directly into Ground Zero and work directly on a pile of debris to help in the search. They were needed on the perimeters of the area to do all the other tasks that fall on the shoulders of police.

"Most of us wanted to be there and help, I mean everybody I know. Every police officer I know wanted to be there and actually help on a pile. Unfortunately that's not what the job requires. You need guys for traffic. You need to secure the perimeter. That was before the National Guard was called out. So a lot of guys were disappointed because they weren't able to be on a pile," explained Ottolia.

All rescue workers told of the horror of finding nothing except body parts or just scraps of human flesh. The scene was more gruesome than any horror movie. But they had to find inner strength to face this ghoulish part of the task.

"I was able to be there and work on the pile," said Ottolia. "When we started pulling out pieces of bodies it was unbelievable. For the past few days I've been over at the landfill. We've been sifting through debris there. You know sometimes you don't find too much, but last night I found a guy's scalp with an ear. That's about all they're finding.

Dogs were used to help locate thousands of body parts buried in the dust and rubble.

"I know they don't want people to say that. They don't want people to know about it, but that's all they're really finding. Tiny bits and pieces. And a lot of it's being found because of the dogs. They're bringing in the K-9s. They're able to sniff out cadavers. And that's how they're coming up with it. Otherwise it's very difficult, because you're not seeing anything that really resembles a human. And when you come across something it's not very recognizable.

"I found the piece of scalp because I came across some debris, looked, and thought to myself that this could be something. But it was mixed in with a lot of dirt, a lot of other things. Then I picked it up and it started to make some sense. Other people helped to identify that is was a piece of a body. They said, 'Oh yeah. That's what you're looking at,'

"It was a day I probably never will forget," Ottolia said.

Thousands of people escaped the towers and nearby buildings because of the fast work of firefighters, the Port Authority, police, and other rescuers. When they first stepped out of the buildings after the initial attack, they were standing on the Plaza and in the streets just looking up at the spectacle of the burning towers. Only after the south tower collapsed did survivors flee the area.

It began with a mad dash to find safety from the debris crashing down all around them. After the towers collapsed they started to leave the area. The injured began finding their way to hospitals for treatment. Those who escaped without injury just wanted to go home to safety, but getting home was a problem. Transportation systems were all down. Most New Yorkers rely on public transportation, so when buses, taxis, and subway trains stop, the only way to travel is on foot.

Thus the mass exodus began. Thousands upon thousands walked for miles to get out of Manhattan, even if their direction was not the way home. They just wanted to get out. And while thousands were trying to get out, rescue workers were trying to find ways in.

Brooklyn Police Department patrolman Brian Bliss was one of those peace officers assigned somewhere other than Ground Zero. Bliss was helping people who escaped the devastation to find their way out of hell and back to the real world.

"I didn't get to see the terror first hand," Bliss explained. "Most of the people I encountered had been at Ground Zero and were walking out. I saw them on the Brooklyn side a few hours after it happened. They had been walking for four hours. The look on these peoples' faces was absolutely amazing."

They had walked from Manhattan into Brooklyn. The trip was long, and many were in poor physical shape. They became dehydrated, were covered in dust from the debris, and felt shell-shocked. Many were dazed, just walking and walking. For a crowd so large, very little talking was heard.

"They looked like zombies," said Bliss. "No expression on their faces. Just a blank stare. People walked around in awe from the awful events. Now, however, they were walking in an unfamiliar town. They're accustomed to going from the financial district uptown to the trains that carried them home. Now they're walking around Brooklyn, and there's no trains even to get them where they need to go to get home. No trains. No buses. They're just winging it, and not exactly in the best parts of Brooklyn. Not a ghetto, but it's a crime-riddled area. And they're walking around aimlessly. We were just trying to get them to where they wanted to go as quickly as possible.

"They all had a long, long day they'll never forget, I'm sure," Bliss added.

Even though there has been tragic loss of life and destruction of property, Bliss said he has already seen good come from the bad.

"It's too bad it takes a tragedy like this to bring everybody together. At least the whole country's sticking together. And there seems to one general consensus. I was driving past our church the other day and it was jammed. I haven't seen it that crowded except for Christmas Eve mass. On a regular Sunday it would never be this crowded," said Bliss.

Both Ottolia and Bliss commented that they expect more trouble before the war on terrorism is over. They said they expect the U.S. to prevail by rounding up the terrorists all over the world.

"I don't think a prompt military response is the answer," said Ottolia. "You would think being in law enforcement we would think 'Go and get em.' But I don't think that's the answer. I think we need a long campaign. Infiltration. Getting cooperation. Weeding them out. You're making martyrs if you go in there and kill, which we don't want to do. For every guy you kill there's going to be two that take his place. They're going to do it willingly. To them it's an honor to die in a holy war against the United States.

"I'm angry because they have no value for human life. That's apparent because any religious zealots who would go and die for what they believe in like that, they really can't have too much respect for other lives either," he added.

Ottolia, a Brooklyn detective hardened by dealing with the worst of our society, said the terrorists should be rounded up in similar fashion to a raid on suspected drug dealers.

"We have the sophistication and technology, and we can go about it differently," he explained. "Let's weed them out. Let's use operatives. You know we had a really strong CIA network years ago. For some reason our government decided that wasn't necessary. Maybe they didn't want them to be that strong. Maybe we should put them back in action," he suggested.

Like Rumson Police Department patrolman Jim Fenn, Ottolia said he does not see any indication that police and firefighters will leave their jobs after the exposure they've had to so much devastation. He also said the people of New York City have a new respect and appreciation for the men and women in uniform who protect them.

First responders faced their greatest nightmare with courage and determination.

"The police and firemen of the city have been doing a great job for years and years and years. It takes something like this for people all of a sudden to realize that. Kinda sad," he said.

"I hope the unity that's been formed, the togetherness and the patriotism, that this has awakened in all of us lingers. Job-wise, I hope that the city finally appreciates the job that we've done. That's why it's been a safe city. That's why the firemen have always done their job.

"We've done our job, but it's been overlooked. I'm hoping now that they finally get the idea and say, 'You know what? These guys have been doing this all along, and it just took something like this for us to realize it.'"

Police and firefighters all over America put their lives on the line every day. They sacrifice to do these jobs, because they get paid far less than they should…far less than they could earn elsewhere. They work terrible hours. They miss out on important family events and activities. They subject themselves to criticism and abuse. They risk death and painful injury every day, and their spouses live with constant fear of what might happen. These brave men and women are the ones, to paraphrase the poet Rudyard Kipling, who guard us while we sleep.

Let's pray Ottolia is right – that after this wake-up call from hell Americans will reappraise how much we value, respect, and pay the people we depend upon to protect public safety in this time of growing danger.

Men like William Cahill, Timothy Hubbard, Bob Balchunis, James Fenn, Maurice Ottolia, Brian Bliss, Pat O'Flaherty and the many others just like them are not looking for a pat on the back. When we meet first responders and military service members we should not hesitate to thank them. We should tell our elected leaders to put a higher priority on increasing the salaries and benefits for the military, police, firefighters, EMS and all first responders throughout our nation.

Chapter 6

Honor Roll

These are the names on the 911 Memorial panels with the location of each name (N for north pool, S for south pool, and panel number). This is the most updated list available and contains names that were not available when the first edition of this book was published. (The audio book version does not include this list of names. Please refer to the print or Kindle version. Kindle readers please continue to the last page.)

Gordon M. Aamoth, Jr. S-49
Edelmiro Abad S-40
Marie Rose Abad S-34
Andrew Anthony Abate N-57
Vincent Paul Abate N-57
Laurence Christopher Abel N-32
Alona Abraham S-4
William F. Abrahamson N-7
Richard Anthony Aceto N-4
Heinrich Bernhard Ackermann S-55
Paul Acquaviva N-37
Christian Adams S-68
Donald LaRoy Adams N-55
Patrick Adams S-45
Shannon Lewis Adams N-49
Stephen George Adams N-70
Ignatius Udo Adanga N-71
Christy A. Addamo N-8
Terence Edward Adderley, Jr. N-58
Sophia B. Addo N-68
Lee Adler N-37
Daniel Thomas Afflitto N-25
Emmanuel Akwasi Afuakwah N-71
Alok Agarwal N-36
Mukul Kumar Agarwala S-43
Joseph Agnello S-11
David Scott Agnes N-47
Joao Alberto da Fonseca Aguiar, Jr. S-34
Brian G. Ahearn S-13
Jeremiah Joseph Ahern S-47
Joanne Marie Ahladiotis N-37
Shabbir Ahmed N-70
Terrance Andre Aiken N-17
Godwin O. Ajala S-65
Trudi M. Alagero N-5
Andrew Alameno N-52
Margaret Ann Alario S-63
Gary M. Albero S-63

Jon Leslie Albert N-7
Peter Craig Alderman N-21
Jacquelyn Delaine Aldridge- Frederick N-10
David D. Alger N-59
Ernest Alikakos S-47
Edward L. Allegretto N-40
Eric Allen S-21
Joseph Ryan Allen N-41
Richard Dennis Allen S-21
Richard L. Allen N-19
Christopher E. Allingham N-42
Anna S. W. Allison N-2
Janet Marie Alonso N-5
Anthony Alvarado N-23
Antonio Javier Alvarez N-70
Victoria Alvarez-Brito N-8
Telmo E. Alvear N-71
Cesar Amoranto Alviar N-16
Tariq Amanullah S-42
Angelo Amaranto N-64
James M. Amato S-7
Joseph Amatuccio S-24
Paul W. Ambrose S-70
Christopher Charles Amoroso S-28
Craig Scott Amundson S-74
Kazuhiro Anai N-63
Calixto Anaya, Jr. S-21
Joseph P. Anchundia S-52
Kermit Charles Anderson N-9
Yvette Constance Anderson S-48
John Jack Andreacchio S-44
Michael Rourke Andrews N-53
Jean Ann Andrucki N-66
Siew-Nya Ang N-5
Joseph Angelini, Sr. S-9
Joseph John Angelini, Jr. S-9
David Lawrence Angell N-1
Mary Lynn Edwards Angell N-1

Laura Angilletta N-32
Doreen J. Angrisani N-15
Lorraine Antigua N-53
Seima David Aoyama N-2
Peter Paul Apollo N-26
Faustino Apostol, Jr. S-6
Frank Thomas Aquilino N-39
Patrick Michael Aranyos S-30
David Gregory Arce S-13
Michael George Arczynski S-54
Louis Arena S-5
Barbara Jean Arestegui N-74
Adam P. Arias S-31
Michael J. Armstrong N-43
Jack Charles Aron N-4
Joshua Todd Aron N-42
Richard Avery Aronow N-66
Myra Joy Aronson N-74
Japhet Jesse Aryee S-48
Carl Francis Asaro S-10
Michael A. Asciak N-63
Michael Edward Asher N-36
Janice Marie Ashley N-58
Thomas J. Ashton N-19
Manuel O. Asitimbay N-68
Gregg A. Atlas S-5
Gerald Thomas Atwood S-11
James Audiffred N-64
Louis F. Aversano, Jr. S-58
Ezra Aviles N-65
Sandy Ayala N-70
Arlene T. Babakitis N-66
Eustace R. Bacchus N-71
John J. Badagliacca N-52
Jane Ellen Baeszler N-43
Robert J. Baierwalter S-63
Andrew J. Bailey N-12
Brett T. Bailey S-31
Garnet Ace Bailey S-3
Tatyana Bakalinskaya N-17
Michael S. Baksh N-16
Sharon M. Balkcom N-7
Michael Andrew Bane N-14
Katherine Bantis N-12
Gerard Baptiste S-14
Walter Baran S-40
Gerard A. Barbara S-18
Paul Vincent Barbaro N-36
James William Barbella S-26
Victor Daniel Barbosa S-37
Christine Johnna Barbuto N-1
Colleen Ann Barkow N-32
David Michael Barkway N-42
Matthew Barnes S-21
Melissa Rose Barnes S-72
Sheila Patricia Barnes S-58
Evan Jay Baron N-60
Renee Barrett-Arjune N-48

Arthur Thaddeus Barry S-20
Diane G. Barry S-56
Maurice Vincent Barry S-28
Scott D. Bart N-9
Carlton W. Bartels N-50
Guy Barzvi N-48
Inna B. Basina N-48
Alysia Christine Burton Basmajian N-47
Kenneth William Basnicki N-21
Steven Joseph Bates S-6
Paul James Battaglia N-4
W. David Bauer N-37
Ivhan Luis Carpio Bautista N-69
Marlyn Capito Bautista N-6
Mark Lawrence Bavis S-3
Jasper Baxter S-45
Lorraine G. Bay S-67
Michele Beale N-20
Todd M. Beamer S-68
Paul Frederick Beatini S-63
Jane S. Beatty N-9
Alan Anthony Beaven S-67
Lawrence Ira Beck N-31
Manette Marie Beckles S-42
Carl John Bedigian S-21
Michael Ernest Beekman S-48
Maria A. Behr N-27
Max J. Beilke S-1
Yelena Belilovsky N-61
Nina Patrice Bell N-8
Debbie S. Bellows N-37
Stephen Elliot Belson S-17
Paul M. Benedetti S-62
Denise Lenore Benedetto S-60
Bryan Craig Bennett N-55
Eric L. Bennett N-65
Oliver Bennett N-20
Margaret L. Benson N-66
Dominick J. Berardi N-31
James Patrick Berger S-56
Steven Howard Berger S-48
John P. Bergin S-6
Alvin Bergsohn N-25
Daniel David Bergstein N-66
Graham Andrew Berkeley S-3
Michael J. Berkeley N-67
Donna M. Bernaerts N-16
David W. Bernard S-66
William H. Bernstein N-56
David M. Berray N-20
David Shelby Berry S-36
Joseph John Berry S-36
William Reed Bethke N-10
Yeneneh Betru S-69
Timothy D. Betterly N-41
Carolyn Mayer Beug N-1
Edward Frank Beyea N-65
Paul Michael Beyer S-14

Anil Tahilram Bharvaney N-22
Bella J. Bhukhan N-49
Shimmy D. Biegeleisen S-42
Peter Alexander Bielfeld S-18
William G. Biggart S-66
Brian Eugene Bilcher S-14
Mark Bingham S-67
Carl Vincent Bini S-6
Gary Eugene Bird N-13
Joshua David Birnbaum N-42
George John Bishop S-59
Kris Romeo Bishundat S-72
Jeffrey Donald Bittner S-35
Albert Balewa Blackman, Jr. N-48
Christopher Joseph Blackwell S-15
Carrie Rosetta Blagburn S-1
Susan Leigh Blair S-56
Harry Blanding, Jr. S-62
Janice Lee Blaney N-16
Craig Michael Blass N-28
Rita Blau S-41
Richard Middleton Blood, Jr. S-62
Michael Andrew Boccardi N-59
John Paul Bocchi N-46
Michael L. Bocchino S-19
Susan M. Bochino S-62
Deora Frances Bodley S-68
Bruce Douglas Boehm N-41
Mary Catherine Murphy Boffa N-3
Nicholas Andrew Bogdan N-13
Darren Christopher Bohan S-56
Lawrence Francis Boisseau S-23
Vincent M. Boland, Jr. N-10
Touri Hamzavi Bolourchi S-4
Alan Bondarenko S-65
Andre Bonheur, Jr. N-58
Colin Arthur Bonnett N-14
Frank J. Bonomo S-12
Yvonne Lucia Bonomo N-18
Sean Booker, Sr. N-19
Kelly Ann Booms N-1
Canfield D. Boone S-74
Mary Jane Booth S-69
Sherry Ann Bordeaux S-42
Krystine Bordenabe S-34
Jerry J. Borg S-66
Martin Michael Boryczewski N-26
Richard Edward Bosco N-58
Klaus Bothe S-3
Carol Marie Bouchard N-75
J. Howard Boulton S-31
Francisco Eligio Bourdier S-38
Thomas Harold Bowden, Jr. N-26
Donna M. Bowen S-75
Kimberly S. Bowers N-36
Veronique Nicole Bowers N-70
Larry Bowman S-65
Shawn Edward Bowman, Jr. N-49

Kevin L. Bowser N-16
Gary R. Box S-6
Gennady Boyarsky N-18
Pamela Boyce N-58
Allen P. Boyle S-73
Michael Boyle S-13
Alfred J. Braca N-41
Sandra Conaty Brace N-18
Kevin Hugh Bracken S-15
Sandy Waugh Bradshaw S-67
David Brian Brady N-22
Alexander Braginsky N-22
Nicholas W. Brandemarti S-33
Daniel Raymond Brandhorst S-4
David Reed Gamboa Brandhorst S-4
Michelle Renee Bratton N-34
Patrice Braut N-10
Lydia Estelle Bravo N-11
Ronald Michael Breitweiser S-42
Edward A. Brennan III N-53
Frank H. Brennan N-55
Michael E. Brennan S-10
Peter Brennan S-8
Thomas More Brennan S-52
Daniel J. Brethel S-17
Gary Lee Bright S-64
Jonathan Eric Briley N-68
Mark A. Brisman S-45
Paul Gary Bristow N-20
Marion R. Britton S-67
Mark Francis Broderick N-28
Herman Charles Broghammer S-58
Keith A. Broomfield N-64
Bernard C. Brown II S-70
Janice Juloise Brown N-11
Lloyd Stanford Brown N-29
Patrick John Brown S-8
Bettina B. Browne-Radburn S-61
Mark Bruce S-52
Richard George Bruehert N-5
Andrew Brunn S-6
Vincent Edward Brunton S-20
Ronald Bucca S-14
Brandon J. Buchanan N-29
Greg J. Buck S-12
Dennis Buckley N-43
Nancy Clare Bueche S-61
Patrick Joseph Buhse N-53
John Edward Bulaga, Jr. N-34
Stephen Bruce Bunin N-37
Christopher L. Burford S-71
Matthew J. Burke N-29
Thomas Daniel Burke N-54
William Francis Burke, Jr. S-18
Charles F. Burlingame III S-69
Thomas E. Burnett, Jr. S-68
Donald J. Burns S-18
Kathleen Anne Burns S-43

Keith James Burns N-28
John Patrick Burnside S-12
Irina Buslo S-44
Milton G. Bustillo N-34
Thomas M. Butler S-7
Patrick Dennis Byrne S-8
Timothy G. Byrne S-50
Daniel M. Caballero S-72
Jesus Neptali Cabezas N-68
Lillian Caceres N-4
Brian Joseph Cachia N-34
Steven Dennis Cafiero, Jr. S-55
Richard Michael Caggiano N-26
Cecile Marella Caguicla N-7
John Brett Cahill S-3
Michael John Cahill N-11
Scott Walter Cahill N-42
Thomas Joseph Cahill N-40
George C. Cain S-20
Salvatore B. Calabro S-8
Joseph M. Calandrillo N-18
Philip V. Calcagno N-15
Edward Calderon S-26
Jose O. Calderon-Olmedo S-74
Kenneth Marcus Caldwell N-65
Dominick E. Calia N-43
Felix Bobby Calixte N-73
Francis Joseph Callahan S-17
Liam Callahan S-29
Suzanne M. Calley S-71
Gino Luigi Calvi N-51
Roko Camaj S-37
Michael F. Cammarata S-15
David Otey Campbell S-34
Geoffrey Thomas Campbell N-22
Robert Arthur Campbell S-44
Sandra Patricia Campbell N-37
Sean Thomas Canavan S-64
John A. Candela N-26
Vincent A. Cangelosi N-41
Stephen J. Cangialosi N-43
Lisa Bella Cannava N-58
Brian Cannizzaro S-8
Michael R. Canty N-61
Louis Anthony Caporicci N-53
Jonathan Neff Cappello N-52
James Christopher Cappers N-15
Richard Michael Caproni N-10
Jose Manuel Cardona N-62
Dennis M. Carey, Sr. S-7
Edward Carlino N-11
Michael Scott Carlo S-12
David G. Carlone S-63
Rosemarie C. Carlson N-67
Mark Stephen Carney N-65
Joyce Ann Carpeneto N-72
Jeremy Caz Carrington N-45
Michael T. Carroll S-8

Peter J. Carroll S-6
James Joseph Carson, Jr. N-35
Christoffer Mikael Carstanjen S-3
Angelene C. Carter S-76
James Marcel Cartier S-64
Sharon Ann Carver S-1
Vivian Casalduc N-65
John Francis Casazza N-52
Paul Regan Cascio S-30
Neilie Anne Heffernan Casey N-75
William Joseph Cashman S-68
Thomas Anthony Casoria S-18
William Otto Caspar N-13
Alejandro Castaño S-38
Arcelia Castillo N-5
Leonard M. Castrianno N-44
Jose Ramon Castro N-23
William E. Caswell S-70
Richard G. Catarelli N-9
Christopher Sean Caton N-54
Robert John Caufield N-19
Mary Teresa Caulfield N-9
Judson Cavalier S-52
Michael Joseph Cawley S-11
Jason David Cayne N-43
Juan Armando Ceballos S-37
Marcia G. Cecil-Carter N-63
Jason Michael Cefalu N-56
Thomas Joseph Celic N-12
Ana Mercedes Centeno N-14
Joni Cesta S-38
John J. Chada S-1
Jeffrey Marc Chairnoff S-51
Swarna Chalasani S-42
William A. Chalcoff N-16
Eli Chalouh S-48
Charles Lawrence Chan N-44
Mandy Chang S-44
Rosa Maria Chapa S-71
Mark Lawrence Charette N-4
David M. Charlebois S-69
Gregorio Manuel Chavez N-70
Pedro Francisco Checo S-39
Douglas MacMillan Cherry S-60
Stephen Patrick Cherry N-26
Vernon Paul Cherry S-11
Nestor Julio Chevalier, Jr. N-33
Swede Joseph Chevalier N-28
Alexander H. Chiang N-10
Dorothy J. Chiarchiaro N-58
Luis Alfonso Chimbo N-70
Robert Chin S-39
Eddie Wing-Wai Ching N-23
Nicholas Paul Chiofalo S-7
John G. Chipura S-21
Peter A. Chirchirillo N-5
Catherine Ellen Chirls N-55
Kyung Hee Casey Cho N-14

Abul K. Chowdhury N-36
Mohammad Salahuddin Chowdhury N-67
Kirsten Lail Christophe S-54
Pamela Chu N-29
Steven Paul Chucknick S-31
Wai Ching Chung S-53
Christopher Ciafardini N-60
Alex F. Ciccone N-8
Frances Ann Cilente N-37
Elaine Cillo N-6
Patricia Ann Cimaroli Massari and her
unborn child N-11
Edna Cintron N-12
Nestor Andre Cintron III N-44
Robert D. Cirri, Sr. S-29
Juan Pablo Cisneros N-52
Benjamin Keefe Clark S-39
Eugene Clark S-56
Gregory Alan Clark N-31
Mannie Leroy Clark N-10
Sara M. Clark S-70
Thomas R. Clark S-51
Christopher Robert Clarke S-50
Donna Marie Clarke N-14
Michael J. Clarke S-16
Suria Rachel Emma Clarke N-34
Kevin Francis Cleary S-32
James D. Cleere N-5
Geoffrey W. Cloud N-47
Susan Marie Clyne N-8
Steven Coakley S-13
Jeffrey Alan Coale N-69
Patricia A. Cody N-8
Daniel Michael Coffey N-5
Jason Matthew Coffey N-5
Florence G. Cohen S-47
Kevin S. Cohen N-33
Anthony Joseph Coladonato N-36
Mark Joseph Colaio N-42
Stephen J. Colaio N-42
Christopher Michael Colasanti N-53
Kevin Nathaniel Colbert S-35
Michel P. Colbert N-52
Keith E. Coleman N-30
Scott Thomas Coleman N-30
Tarel Coleman S-23
Liam Joseph Colhoun N-73
Robert D. Colin S-61
Robert J. Coll S-31
Jean Marie Collin S-63
John Michael Collins S-22
Michael L. Collins N-36
Thomas Joseph Collins S-50
Joseph Kent Collison N-72
Jeffrey Dwayne Collman N-74
Patricia Malia Colodner N-6
Linda M. Colon N-3
Sol E. Colon S-58

Ronald Edward Comer N-11
Jaime Concepcion N-70
Albert Conde S-63
Denease Conley S-65
Susan P. Conlon N-73
Margaret Mary Conner N-31
Cynthia Marie Lise Connolly S-56
John E. Connolly, Jr. S-32
James Lee Connor S-50
Jonathan M. Connors N-25
Kevin Patrick Connors S-30
Kevin F. Conroy N-4
Brenda E. Conway N-12
Dennis Michael Cook N-40
Helen D. Cook N-72
Jeffrey W. Coombs N-2
John A. Cooper S-49
Julian T. Cooper S-73
Joseph John Coppo, Jr. N-43
Gerard J. Coppola N-63
Joseph Albert Corbett N-53
John J. Corcoran III S-4
Alejandro Cordero N-6
Robert Joseph Cordice S-7
Ruben D. Correa S-9
Danny A. Correa-Gutierrez N-7
Georgine Rose Corrigan S-68
James J. Corrigan, Ret. S-5
Carlos Cortés-Rodriguez S-65
Kevin Michael Cosgrove S-60
Dolores Marie Costa N-58
Digna Alexandra Costanza N-13
Charles Gregory Costello, Jr. N-64
Michael S. Costello N-26
Asia S. Cottom S-70
Conrod Kofi Cottoy, Sr. N-62
Martin John Coughlan S-64
John G. Coughlin S-23
Timothy J. Coughlin N-54
James E. Cove S-59
Andre Colin Cox N-23
Frederick John Cox S-50
James Raymond Coyle S-7
Michele Coyle-Eulau N-11
Christopher Seton Cramer S-42
Eric A. Cranford S-72
Denise Elizabeth Crant N-10
James Leslie Crawford, Jr. N-27
Robert James Crawford S-18
Tara Kathleen Creamer N-75
Joanne Mary Cregan N-37
Lucia Crifasi N-18
John A. Crisci S-8
Daniel Hal Crisman N-15
Dennis A. Cross S-6
Kevin R. Crotty S-52
Thomas G. Crotty S-53
John R. Crowe S-55

Welles Remy Crowther S-50
Robert L. Cruikshank N-58
John Robert Cruz N-49
Grace Alegre Cua S-39
Kenneth John Cubas S-43
Francisco Cruz Cubero S-65
Thelma Cuccinello N-1
Richard Joseph Cudina N-51
Neil James Cudmore N-20
Thomas Patrick Cullen III S-13
Joan Cullinan N-31
Joyce Rose Cummings S-39
Brian Thomas Cummins N-27
Michael Joseph Cunningham S-31
Robert Curatolo S-19
Laurence Damian Curia N-41
Paul Dario Curioli S-63
Patrick Joseph Currivan N-74
Beverly L. Curry N-35
Andrew Peter Charles Curry Green N-1
Michael Sean Curtin S-24
Patricia Cushing S-67
Gavin Cushny N-31
Caleb Arron Dack N-21
Carlos S. da Costa S-25
Jason M. Dahl S-67
Brian Paul Dale N-76
John D'Allara S-24
Vincent Gerard D'Amadeo N-32
Thomas A. Damaskinos N-32
Jack L. D'Ambrosi, Jr. N-45
Jeannine Damiani-Jones N-42
Manuel João DaMota N-71
Patrick W. Danahy S-40
Mary D'Antonio N-6
Vincent G. Danz S-24
Dwight Donald Darcy N-66
Elizabeth Ann Darling N-12
Annette Andrea Dataram N-69
Edward A. D'Atri S-6
Michael D. D'Auria S-16
Lawrence Davidson S-62
Michael Allen Davidson N-30
Scott Matthew Davidson S-10
Titus Davidson S-46
Niurka Davila N-66
Ada M. Davis S-75
Clinton Davis, Sr. S-28
Wayne Terrial Davis N-21
Anthony Richard Dawson N-22
Calvin Dawson S-32
Edward James Day S-15
William Thomas Dean N-11
Robert J. DeAngelis, Jr. S-64
Thomas Patrick DeAngelis S-16
Dorothy Alma de Araujo S-4
Ana Gloria Pocasangre Debarrera S-2
Tara E. Debek N-9

James D. Debeuneure S-70
Anna M. DeBin N-47
James V. DeBlase, Jr. N-51
Jayceryll Malabuyoc de Chavez S-40
Paul DeCola N-36
Gerald F. DeConto S-72
Simon Marash Dedvukaj N-64
Jason Christopher DeFazio N-40
David A. DeFeo S-49
Jennifer De Jesus S-46
Monique Effie DeJesus N-29
Nereida De Jesus S-60
Emy De La Peña S-40
Donald Arthur Delapenha S-36
Azucena Maria de la Torre N-47
Vito Joseph DeLeo N-63
Danielle Anne Delie N-3
Joseph A. Della Pietra N-40
Andrea DellaBella S-58
Palmina DelliGatti N-4
Colleen Ann Deloughery S-59
Joseph DeLuca S-68
Manuel Del Valle, Jr. S-16
Francis Albert De Martini S-27
Anthony Demas S-55
Martin N. DeMeo S-9
Francis Deming N-17
Carol Keyes Demitz S-42
Kevin Dennis N-44
Thomas Francis Dennis, Sr. N-56
Jean C. DePalma N-12
Jose Nicolas De Pena N-69
Robert John Deraney N-21
Michael DeRienzo N-53
David Paul DeRubbio S-14
Jemal Legesse DeSantis N-58
Christian Louis DeSimone N-4
Edward DeSimone III N-53
Andrew J. Desperito S-18
Michael Jude D'Esposito N-6
Cindy Ann Deuel N-59
Melanie Louise de Vere N-20
Jerry DeVito N-60
Robert P. Devitt, Jr. N-32
Dennis Lawrence Devlin S-15
Gerard P. Dewan S-8
Sulemanali Kassamali Dhanani S-53
Michael Louis DiAgostino N-49
Matthew Diaz N-24
Nancy Diaz N-70
Obdulio Ruiz Diaz N-71
Michael A. Diaz-Piedra III N-72
Judith Berquis Diaz-Sierra S-40
Patricia Florence Di Chiaro N-8
Rodney Dickens S-70
Jerry D. Dickerson S-74
Joseph Dermot Dickey, Jr. N-46
Lawrence Patrick Dickinson N-67

Michael D. Diehl S-40
John Difato N-58
Vincent Francis DiFazio N-55
Carl Anthony DiFranco N-4
Donald Joseph DiFranco N-64
John DiGiovanni N-73
Eddie A. Dillard S-70
Debra Ann Di Martino S-36
David DiMeglio N-2
Stephen Patrick Dimino N-53
William John Dimmling N-12
Christopher More Dincuff N-60
Jeffrey Mark Dingle N-21
Rena Sam Dinnoo N-12
Anthony Dionisio N-33
George DiPasquale S-17
Joseph Di Pilato S-46
Douglas Frank DiStefano N-49
Donald Americo DiTullio N-75
Ramzi A. Doany N-14
Johnnie Doctor, Jr. S-72
John Joseph Doherty S-60
Melissa Cándida Doi S-46
Brendan Dolan N-61
Robert E. Dolan, Jr. S-73
Neil Matthew Dollard N-40
James Domanico S-48
Benilda Pascua Domingo S-37
Alberto Dominguez N-2
Carlos Dominguez N-3
Jerome Mark Patrick Dominguez S-25
Kevin W. Donnelly S-6
Jacqueline Donovan S-33
William H. Donovan S-73
Stephen Scott Dorf S-32
Thomas Dowd N-55
Kevin Christopher Dowdell S-11
Mary Yolanda Dowling S-59
Raymond Matthew Downey, Sr. S-9
Frank Joseph Doyle S-34
Joseph Michael Doyle N-33
Randall L. Drake S-38
Patrick Joseph Driscoll S-68
Stephen Patrick Driscoll S-24
Charles A. Droz III S-70
Mirna A. Duarte N-16
Luke A. Dudek N-70
Christopher Michael Duffy S-35
Gerard J. Duffy S-10
Michael Joseph Duffy S-35
Thomas W. Duffy N-4
Antoinette Duger N-72
Jackie Sayegh Duggan N-69
Sareve Dukat S-48
Patrick Dunn S-72
Felicia Gail Dunn-Jones S-66
Christopher Joseph Dunne N-13
Richard Anthony Dunstan S-59

Patrick Thomas Dwyer N-25
Joseph Anthony Eacobacci N-50
John Bruce Eagleson S-66
Edward T. Earhart S-72
Robert Douglas Eaton N-46
Dean Phillip Eberling S-33
Margaret Ruth Echtermann S-48
Paul Robert Eckna N-28
Constantine Economos S-51
Barbara G. Edwards S-70
Dennis Michael Edwards N-54
Michael Hardy Edwards S-50
Christine Egan S-53
Lisa Erin Egan N-49
Martin J. Egan, Jr. S-11
Michael Egan S-53
Samantha Martin Egan N-49
Carole Eggert N-6
Lisa Caren Ehrlich S-62
John Ernst Eichler N-71
Eric Adam Eisenberg S-58
Daphne Ferlinda Elder N-8
Michael J. Elferis S-18
Mark Joseph Ellis S-25
Valerie Silver Ellis N-25
Albert Alfy William Elmarry N-36
Robert R. Elseth S-73
Edgar Hendricks Emery, Jr. S-41
Doris Suk-Yuen Eng N-70
Christopher Epps N-6
Ulf Ramm Ericson S-65
Erwin L. Erker N-5
William John Erwin N-46
Sarah Ali Escarcega N-20
Jose Espinal S-66
Fanny Espinoza N-47
Billy Scoop Esposito N-40
Bridget Ann Esposito N-18
Francis Esposito S-7
Michael A. Esposito S-7
Ruben Esquilin, Jr. S-39
Sadie Ette N-69
Barbara G. Etzold N-59
Eric Brian Evans S-59
Robert Edward Evans S-15
Meredith Emily June Ewart S-54
Catherine K. Fagan N-13
Patricia Mary Fagan S-55
Ivan Kyrillos Fairbanks-Barbosa N-43
Keith George Fairben S-26
Sandra Fajardo-Smith N-7
Charles S. Falkenberg S-69
Dana Falkenberg S-69
Zoe Falkenberg S-69
Jamie L. Fallon S-72
William F. Fallon N-65
William Lawrence Fallon, Jr. N-37
Anthony J. Fallone, Jr. N-51

Dolores Brigitte Fanelli N-5
Robert John Fangman S-2
John Joseph Fanning S-11
Kathleen Anne Faragher N-22
Thomas James Farino S-19
Nancy C. Doloszycki Farley N-18
Paige Marie Farley-Hackel N-75
Elizabeth Ann Farmer N-47
Douglas Jon Farnum N-10
John Gerard Farrell N-53
John W. Farrell S-51
Terrence Patrick Farrell S-11
Joseph D. Farrelly S-22
Thomas Patrick Farrelly N-17
Syed Abdul Fatha S-49
Christopher Edward Faughnan N-54
Wendy R. Faulkner S-61
Shannon Marie Fava N-35
Bernard D. Favuzza N-42
Robert Fazio, Jr. S-24
Ronald Carl Fazio, Sr. S-60
William M. Feehan S-18
Francis Jude Feely N-7
Garth Erin Feeney N-21
Sean Bernard Fegan N-60
Lee S. Fehling S-7
Peter Adam Feidelberg S-54
Alan D. Feinberg S-10
Rosa Maria Feliciano N-15
Edward P. Felt S-68
Edward Thomas Fergus, Jr. N-41
George J. Ferguson III S-37
J. Joseph Ferguson S-69
Henry Fernandez N-70
Judy Hazel Santillan Fernandez N-36
Julio Fernandez S-45
Elisa Giselle Ferraina N-20
Anne Marie Sallerin Ferreira N-44
Robert John Ferris S-60
David Francis Ferrugio N-56
Louis V. Fersini, Jr. N-43
Michael David Ferugio S-63
Bradley James Fetchet S-35
Jennifer Louise Fialko S-59
Kristen Nicole Fiedel N-6
Amelia V. Fields S-75
Samuel Fields S-65
Alexander Milan Filipov N-2
Michael Bradley Finnegan N-45
Timothy J. Finnerty N-52
Michael C. Fiore S-5
Stephen J. Fiorelli N-66
Paul M. Fiori N-24
John B. Fiorito N-41
John R. Fischer S-13
Andrew Fisher N-22
Bennett Lawson Fisher S-40
Gerald P. Fisher S-75

John Roger Fisher N-66
Thomas J. Fisher S-41
Lucy A. Fishman S-61
Ryan D. Fitzgerald S-40
Thomas James Fitzpatrick S-52
Richard P. Fitzsimons S-23
Salvatore Fiumefreddo N-24
Darlene E. Flagg S-70
Wilson F. Flagg S-70
Christina Donovan Flannery S-50
Eileen Flecha S-41
Andre G. Fletcher S-7
Carl M. Flickinger N-40
Matthew M. Flocco S-72
John Joseph Florio S-22
Joseph Walkden Flounders S-32
Carol Ann Flyzik N-1
David Fodor S-41
Michael N. Fodor S-11
Stephen Mark Fogel N-47
Thomas J. Foley S-16
Jane C. Folger S-67
David J. Fontana S-6
Chih Min Foo S-44
Delrose E. Forbes Cheatham N-48
Godwin Forde S-46
Donald A. Foreman S-27
Christopher Hugh Forsythe N-44
Claudia Alicia Foster N-56
Noel John Foster S-62
Sandra N. Foster S-71
Ana Fosteris S-61
Robert Joseph Foti S-20
Jeffrey Fox S-35
Virginia Elizabeth Fox N-10
Pauline Francis N-24
Virgin Lucy Francis N-69
Gary Jay Frank S-58
Morton H. Frank N-26
Peter Christopher Frank N-59
Colleen L. Fraser S-68
Richard K. Fraser S-59
Kevin J. Frawley S-33
Clyde Frazier, Jr. S-27
Lillian Inez Frederick S-58
Andrew Fredericks S-21
Tamitha Freeman S-58
Brett Owen Freiman S-46
Peter L. Freund S-7
Arlene Eva Fried N-46
Alan W. Friedlander S-58
Andrew Keith Friedman N-59
Paul J. Friedman N-75
Gregg J. Froehner S-29
Lisa Anne Frost S-3
Peter Christian Fry S-32
Clement A. Fumando N-33
Steven Elliot Furman N-50

Paul James Furmato N-26
Karleton Douglas Beye Fyfe N-1
G Fredric Neal Gabler N-26
Richard Peter Gabriel S-70
Richard S. Gabrielle S-55
James Andrew Gadiel N-31
Pamela Lee Gaff S-55
Ervin Vincent Gailliard S-66
Deanna Lynn Galante and her
unborn child N-37
Grace Catherine Galante N-37
Anthony Edward Gallagher N-50
Daniel James Gallagher N-28
John Patrick Gallagher N-49
Lourdes J. Galletti N-47
Cono E. Gallo N-61
Vincent Gallucci N-5
Thomas E. Galvin N-39
Giovanna Galletta Gambale N-34
Thomas Gambino, Jr. S-15
Giann F. Gamboa S-37
Ronald L. Gamboa S-4
Peter James Ganci, Jr. S-17
Michael Gann N-20
Charles William Garbarini S-12
Andrew Sonny Garcia S-68
Cesar R. Garcia N-5
David Garcia N-17
Jorge Luis Morron Garcia S-65
Juan Garcia N-23
Marlyn Del Carmen Garcia N-3
Christopher Samuel Gardner S-57
Douglas Benjamin Gardner N-38
Harvey Joseph Gardner III N-72
Jeffrey Brian Gardner N-4
Thomas A. Gardner S-8
William Arthur Gardner N-37
Frank Garfi N-25
Rocco Nino Gargano N-28
James M. Gartenberg N-64
Matthew David Garvey S-6
Bruce Gary S-15
Boyd Alan Gatton S-43
Donald Richard Gavagan, Jr. N-42
Peter Alan Gay N-2
Terence D. Gazzani N-51
Gary Paul Geidel S-10
Paul Hamilton Geier N-51
Julie M. Geis S-57
Peter Gerard Gelinas N-56
Steven Paul Geller N-29
Howard G. Gelling, Jr. S-51
Peter Victor Genco, Jr. N-41
Steven Gregory Genovese N-26
Alayne Gentul S-42
Linda M. George N-75
Edward F. Geraghty S-9
Suzanne Geraty N-35

Ralph Gerhardt N-45
Robert Gerlich N-18
Denis P. Germain S-16
Marina Romanovna Gertsberg N-48
Susan M. Getzendanner S-40
Lawrence D. Getzfred S-72
James G. Geyer N-55
Cortez Ghee S-75
Joseph M. Giaccone N-36
Vincent Francis Giammona S-6
Debra Lynn Gibbon S-54
James Andrew Giberson S-16
Brenda C. Gibson S-1
Craig Neil Gibson N-16
Ronnie E. Gies S-8
Andrew Clive Gilbert N-45
Timothy Paul Gilbert N-45
Paul Stuart Gilbey S-32
Paul John Gill S-9
Mark Y. Gilles N-50
Evan Hunter Gillette S-50
Ronald Lawrence Gilligan N-33
Rodney C. Gillis S-24
Laura Gilly N-35
John F. Ginley S-16
Donna Marie Giordano S-55
Jeffrey John Giordano S-8
John Giordano S-18
Steven A. Giorgetti N-13
Martin Giovinazzo N-3
Kum-Kum Girolamo S-54
Salvatore Gitto N-10
Cynthia Giugliano N-64
Mon Gjonbalaj S-37
Dianne Gladstone S-47
Keith Alexander Glascoe S-11
Thomas Irwin Glasser S-49
Edmund Glazer N-75
Harry Glenn N-16
Barry H. Glick N-66
Jeremy Logan Glick S-67
Steven Glick N-21
John T. Gnazzo N-32
William Robert Godshalk S-35
Michael Gogliormella N-35
Brian F. Goldberg S-42
Jeffrey G. Goldflam N-38
Michelle Goldstein S-62
Monica Goldstein N-48
Steven Ian Goldstein N-50
Ronald F. Golinski S-75
Andrew H. Golkin N-46
Dennis James Gomes S-43
Enrique Antonio Gomez N-68
Jose Bienvenido Gomez N-68
Manuel Gomez, Jr. S-44
Wilder Alfredo Gomez N-69
Jenine Nicole Gonzalez S-53

Mauricio Gonzalez S-64
Rosa J. Gonzalez N-66
Lynn Catherine Goodchild S-3
Calvin Joseph Gooding N-39
Peter Morgan Goodrich S-3
Harry Goody S-48
Kiran Kumar Reddy Gopu N-8
Catherine C. Gorayeb N-22
Lisa Fenn Gordenstein N-75
Kerene Gordon N-24
Sebastian Gorki S-38
Kieran Joseph Gorman S-36
Thomas Edward Gorman S-28
Michael Edward Gould N-25
O. Kristin Osterholm White Gould S-68
Douglas Alan Gowell S-4
Yuji Goya S-45
Jon Richard Grabowski N-15
Christopher Michael Grady N-46
Edwin J. Graf III N-41
David Martin Graifman S-34
Gilbert Franco Granados S-58
Lauren Catuzzi Grandcolas and
her unborn child S-68
Elvira Granitto N-64
Winston Arthur Grant N-65
Christopher S. Gray N-44
Ian J. Gray S-71
James Michael Gray S-13
Tara McCloud Gray N-72
John M. Grazioso N-25
Timothy George Grazioso N-25
Derrick Auther Green S-42
Wade B. Green N-23
Wanda Anita Green S-67
Elaine Myra Greenberg N-20
Donald Freeman Greene S-67
Gayle R. Greene N-9
James Arthur Greenleaf, Jr. N-62
Eileen Marsha Greenstein S-56
Elizabeth Martin Gregg N-59
Denise Marie Gregory N-63
Donald H. Gregory N-39
Florence Moran Gregory S-58
Pedro Grehan N-51
John Michael Griffin N-63
Tawanna Sherry Griffin N-23
Joan Donna Griffith S-39
Warren Grifka N-15
Ramon B. Grijalvo N-65
Joseph F. Grillo N-66
David Joseph Grimner N-12
Francis Edward Grogan S-4
Linda Gronlund S-68
Kenneth George Grouzalis S-25
Joseph Grzelak S-19
Matthew James Grzymalski N-54
Robert Joseph Gschaar S-53

Liming Gu N-3
Richard J. Guadagno S-67
Jose A. Guadalupe S-10
Cindy Yan Zhu Guan S-48
Geoffrey E. Guja S-12
Joseph P. Gullickson S-9
Babita Girjamatie Guman S-39
Douglas Brian Gurian N-39
Janet Ruth Gustafson S-61
Philip T. Guza S-53
Barbara Guzzardo S-55
Peter Mark Gyulavary S-65
Gary Robert Haag N-5
Andrea Lyn Haberman N-61
Barbara Mary Habib N-9
Philip Haentzler N-73
Nezam A. Hafiz N-6
Karen Elizabeth Hagerty S-54
Steven Michael Hagis N-55
Mary Lou Hague S-35
David Halderman S-21
Maile Rachel Hale N-21
Diane Hale-McKinzy S-1
Richard B. Hall S-54
Stanley R. Hall S-70
Vaswald George Hall N-67
Robert J. Halligan S-54
Vincent Gerard Halloran S-13
Carolyn B. Halmon S-75
James Douglas Halvorson N-0
Mohammad Salman Hamdani S-66
Felicia Hamilton S-41
Robert W. Hamilton S-12
Carl Max Hammond, Jr. S-3
Frederic K. Han N-46
Christopher James Hanley N-22
Sean S. Hanley S-12
Valerie Joan Hanna N-9
Thomas Paul Hannafin S-5
Kevin James Hannaford, Sr. N-50
Michael Lawrence Hannan N-10
Dana Rey Hannon S-19
Christine Lee Hanson S-4
Peter Burton Hanson S-4
Sue Kim Hanson S-4
Vassilios G. Haramis S-65
James A. Haran N-51
Gerald Francis Hardacre S-4
Jeffrey Pike Hardy N-24
T.J. Hargrave N-55
Daniel Edward Harlin S-16
Frances Haros S-35
Harvey L. Harrell S-5
Stephen G. Harrell S-5
Melissa Harrington-Hughes N-22
Aisha Ann Harris N-72
Stewart D. Harris N-47
John Patrick Hart S-39

Eric Hartono S-4
John Clinton Hartz S-43
Emeric Harvey N-67
Peter Paul Hashem N-2
Thomas Theodore Haskell, Jr. S-22
Timothy Shawn Haskell S-22
Joseph John Hasson III N-55
Leonard W. Hatton, Jr. S-26
Terence S. Hatton S-9
Michael Helmut Haub S-10
Timothy Aaron Haviland N-14
Donald G. Havlish, Jr. S-56
Anthony Maurice Hawkins N-31
Nobuhiro Hayatsu S-39
James Edward Hayden S-4
Robert Jay Hayes N-76
Philip T. Hayes, Ret. S-13
W. Ward Haynes N-49
Scott Jordan Hazelcorn N-54
Michael K. Healey S-12
Roberta B. Heber N-7
Charles Francis Xavier Heeran N-29
John F. Heffernan S-15
Michele M. Heidenberger S-69
Sheila M.S. Hein S-75
H. Joseph Heller, Jr. N-62
JoAnn L. Heltibridle N-14
Ronald John Hemenway S-71
Mark F. Hemschoot S-62
Ronnie Lee Henderson S-23
Brian Hennessey N-35
Edward R. Hennessy, Jr. N-76
Michelle Marie Henrique S-41
Joseph Patrick Henry S-10
William L. Henry, Jr. S-10
Catherina Henry-Robinson N-72
John Christopher Henwood N-52
Robert Allan Hepburn N-14
Mary Herencia S-55
Lindsay C. Herkness III S-46
Harvey Robert Hermer N-24
Norberto Hernandez N-68
Raul Hernandez N-31
Gary Herold S-58
Jeffrey Alan Hersch N-47
Thomas J. Hetzel S-17
Leon Bernard Heyward MC
Sundance S-36
Brian Christopher Hickey S-12
Enemencio Dario Hidalgo Cedeño N-69
Timothy Brian Higgins S-22
Robert D. W. Higley II S-59
Todd Russell Hill S-46
Clara Victorine Hinds N-69
Neal O. Hinds S-37
Mark Hindy N-25
Katsuyuki Hirai S-39
Heather Malia Ho N-70

Tara Yvette Hobbs S-59
Thomas Anderson Hobbs N-50
James J. Hobin N-9
Robert Wayne Hobson III N-49
DaJuan Hodges N-8
Ronald G. Hoerner S-65
Patrick A. Hoey N-66
John A. Hofer N-2
Marcia Hoffman N-36
Stephen Gerard Hoffman N-42
Frederick Joseph Hoffmann N-39
Michele L. Hoffmann N-39
Judith Florence Hofmiller N-16
Wallace Cole Hogan, Jr. S-74
Thomas Warren Hohlweck, Jr. S-60
Jonathan R. Hohmann S-8
Cora Hidalgo Holland N-2
John Holland N-70
Joseph F. Holland N-61
Jimmie I. Holley S-75
Elizabeth Holmes S-32
Thomas P. Holohan S-14
Herbert Wilson Homer S-2
LeRoy W. Homer, Jr. S-67
Bradley V. Hoorn N-58
James P. Hopper N-30
Montgomery McCullough Hord N-29
Michael Joseph Horn N-27
Matthew Douglas Horning N-16
Robert L. Horohoe, Jr. N-39
Michael Robert Horrocks S-2
Aaron Horwitz N-42
Charles J. Houston S-32
Uhuru G. Houston S-28
Angela M. Houtz S-73
George Gerard Howard S-28
Brady Kay Howell S-73
Michael C. Howell N-60
Steven Leon Howell N-3
Jennifer L. Howley and her unborn child S-56
Milagros Hromada S-55
Marian R. Hrycak S-48
Stephen Huczko, Jr. S-30
Kris Robert Hughes S-34
Paul Rexford Hughes N-16
Robert T. Hughes, Jr. N-73
Thomas F. Hughes, Jr. N-71
Timothy Robert Hughes N-44
Susan Huie N-20
Lamar Demetrius Hulse N-17
John Nicholas Humber, Jr. N-1
William Christopher Hunt S-33
Kathleen Anne Hunt-Casey S-50
Joseph Gerard Hunter S-8
Peggie M. Hurt S-75
Robert R. Hussa N-62
Stephen N. Hyland, Jr. S-74
Robert J. Hymel S-71

Thomas Edward Hynes S-37
Walter G. Hynes S-17
Joseph Anthony Ianelli N-9
Zuhtu Ibis N-36
Jonathan Lee Ielpi S-7
Michael Patrick Iken S-33
Daniel Ilkanayev N-48
Frederick J. Ill, Jr. S-16
Abraham Nethanel Ilowitz N-64
Anthony P. Infante, Jr. S-27
Louis S. Inghilterra S-43
Christopher Noble Ingrassia N-30
Paul Innella N-36
Stephanie Veronica Irby N-7
Douglas Jason Irgang S-50
Kristin Irvine-Ryan S-51
Todd Antione Isaac N-56
Erik Hans Isbrandtsen N-25
Taizo Ishikawa S-45
Waleed Joseph Iskandar N-1
Aram Iskenderian, Jr. N-47
John F. Iskyan N-52
Kazushige Ito S-45
Aleksandr Valeryevich Ivantsov N-27
Lacey Bernard Ivory S-74
Virginia May Jablonski N-5
Bryan C. Jack S-70
Brooke Alexandra Jackman N-41
Aaron Jeremy Jacobs N-29
Ariel Louis Jacobs N-21
Jason Kyle Jacobs S-40
Michael G. Jacobs S-42
Steven A. Jacobson N-71
Steven D. Jacoby S-70
Ricknauth Jaggernauth N-71
Jake Denis Jagoda N-34
Yudhvir S. Jain N-37
Maria Jakubiak N-11
Robert Adrien Jalbert S-2
Ernest James N-5
Gricelda E. James N-67
Mark Steven Jardim N-23
Amy Nicole Jarret S-2
Muhammadou Jawara N-70
Francois Jean-Pierre N-71
Maxima Jean-Pierre N-24
Paul Edward Jeffers N-52
John Charles Jenkins N-76
Joseph Jenkins, Jr. S-64
Alan Keith Jensen S-43
Prem Nath Jerath N-67
Farah Jeudy S-60
Hweidar Jian N-27
Eliezer Jimenez, Jr. N-69
Luis Jimenez, Jr. N-13
Charles Gregory John S-45
Nicholas John N-23
Dennis M. Johnson S-74

LaShawna Johnson N-72
Scott Michael Johnson S-33
William R. Johnston S-14
Allison Horstmann Jones S-51
Arthur Joseph Jones III N-59
Brian Leander Jones S-39
Charles Edward Jones N-74
Christopher D. Jones N-41
Donald T. Jones II N-43
Donald W. Jones N-55
Judith Lawter Jones S-73
Linda Jones S-56
Mary S. Jones N-65
Andrew Brian Jordan, Sr. S-22
Robert Thomas Jordan N-42
Albert Gunnis Joseph S-46
Ingeborg Joseph S-46
Karl Henry Joseph S-20
Stephen Joseph S-44
Jane Eileen Josiah S-43
Anthony Jovic S-10
Angel L. Juarbe, Jr. S-16
Karen Sue Juday N-31
Ann C. Judge S-70
Mychal F. Judge S-18
Paul William Jurgens S-30
Thomas Edward Jurgens S-26
Shashikiran Lakshmikantha Kadaba N-18
Gavkharoy Kamardinova S-64
Shari Kandell N-32
Howard Lee Kane N-69
Jennifer Lynn Kane N-4
Vincent D. Kane S-18
Joon Koo Kang N-29
Sheldon Robert Kanter N-36
Deborah H. Kaplan N-66
Robin Lynne Kaplan N-1
Alvin Peter Kappelmann, Jr. S-63
Charles H. Karczewski S-56
William A. Karnes N-9
Douglas Gene Karpiloff S-26
Charles L. Kasper S-11
Andrew K. Kates N-38
John A. Katsimatides N-39
Robert Michael Kaulfers S-28
Don Jerome Kauth, Jr. S-36
Hideya Kawauchi S-44
Edward T. Keane N-66
Richard M. Keane N-15
Lisa Yvonne Kearney-Griffin N-18
Karol Ann Keasler S-34
Barbara A. Keating N-76
Paul Hanlon Keating S-5
Leo Russell Keene III S-33
Brenda Kegler S-1
Chandler Raymond Keller S-69
Joseph John Keller S-46

Peter R. Kellerman N-28
Joseph P. Kellett N-61
Frederick H. Kelley III N-43
James Joseph Kelly N-56
Joseph A. Kelly N-51
Maurice P. Kelly N-24
Richard John Kelly, Jr. S-15
Thomas Michael Kelly S-30
Thomas Richard Kelly S-20
Thomas W. Kelly S-20
Timothy Colin Kelly N-43
William Hill Kelly, Jr. N-21
Robert Clinton Kennedy N-12
Thomas J. Kennedy S-8
Yvonne E. Kennedy S-69
John Richard Keohane S-63
Ralph Francis Kershaw S-3
Ronald T. Kerwin S-8
Howard L. Kestenbaum S-53
Douglas D. Ketcham N-29
Ruth Ellen Ketler S-40
Boris Khalif N-17
Norma Cruz Khan S-71
Sarah Khan N-24
Taimour Firaz Khan N-62
Rajesh Khandelwal N-12
SeiLai Khoo N-59
Michael Vernon Kiefer S-22
Satoshi Kikuchihara S-39
Andrew Jay-Hoon Kim N-60
Lawrence Don Kim N-10
Mary Jo Kimelman N-54
Heinrich Kimmig S-3
Karen Ann Kincaid S-70
Amy R. King S-2
Andrew M. King N-44
Lucille Teresa King S-61
Robert King, Jr. S-14
Lisa King-Johnson S-36
Brian K. Kinney S-3
Takashi Kinoshita S-44
Chris Michael Kirby S-64
Robert Kirkpatrick N-73
Howard Barry Kirschbaum N-8
Glenn Davis Kirwin N-38
Helen Crossin Kittle and her
unborn child N-35
Richard Joseph Klares S-63
Peter Anton Klein N-17
Alan David Kleinberg N-52
Karen Joyce Klitzman N-45
Ronald Philip Kloepfer S-25
Stephen A. Knapp N-73
Eugueni Kniazev N-69
Andrew James Knox N-24
Thomas Patrick Knox N-50
Rebecca Lee Koborie N-4
Deborah A. Kobus S-39

Gary Edward Koecheler S-32
Frank J. Koestner N-28
Ryan Kohart N-27
Vanessa Lynn Przybylo Kolpak S-36
Irina Kolpakova S-45
Suzanne Rose Kondratenko S-63
Abdoulaye Koné N-68
Bon Seok Koo N-73
Dorota Kopiczko N-15
Scott Michael Kopytko S-21
Bojan George Kostic N-27
Danielle Kousoulis N-40
David P. Kovalcin N-2
John J. Kren S-32
William Edward Krukowski S-11
Lyudmila Ksido N-17
Toshiya Kuge S-68
Shekhar Kumar N-35
Kenneth Bruce Kumpel S-22
Frederick Kuo, Jr. S-65
Patricia A. Kuras N-3
Nauka Kushitani S-41
Thomas Joseph Kuveikis S-22
Victor Kwarkye N-68
Raymond Kui Fai Kwok N-33
Angela Reed Kyte N-11
Andrew La Corte N-62
Carol Ann La Plante N-15
Jeffrey G. La Touche N-70
Kathryn L. LaBorie S-2
Amarnauth Lachhman N-24
Ganesh K. Ladkat N-34
James Patrick Ladley N-40
Joseph A. Lafalce N-32
Jeanette Louise Lafond-Menichino N-10
David James LaForge S-12
Michael Patrick LaForte N-53
Alan Charles LaFrance N-69
Juan Mendez Lafuente N-71
Neil Kwong-Wah Lai S-47
Vincent Anthony Laieta S-53
William David Lake S-16
Franco Lalama N-66
Chow Kwan Lam S-48
Michael S. Lamana S-72
Stephen LaMantia N-56
Amy Hope Lamonsoff N-20
Robert T. Lane S-7
Brendan Mark Lang N-26
Rosanne P. Lang N-26
Vanessa Lang Langer and her
unborn child S-49
Mary Lou Langley S-53
Peter J. Langone S-23
Thomas Michael Langone S-23
Michele Bernadette Lanza S-40
Ruth Sheila Lapin S-37
Ingeborg A.D. Lariby S-49

Robin Blair Larkey N-44
Judith Camilla Larocque N-2
Christopher Randall Larrabee N-25
Hamidou S. Larry N-9
Scott Larsen S-21
John Adam Larson S-57
Natalie Janis Lasden N-75
Gary Edward Lasko N-7
Nicholas Craig Lassman N-36
Paul Laszczynski S-29
Charles A. Laurencin S-46
Stephen James Lauria N-7
Maria LaVache N-6
Denis Francis Lavelle N-16
Jeannine Mary LaVerde S-36
Anna A. Laverty S-39
Steven Lawn S-54
Robert A. Lawrence, Jr. S-49
Nathaniel Lawson N-23
David W. Laychak S-1
Eugen Gabriel Lazar N-33
James Patrick Leahy S-25
Joseph Gerard Leavey S-21
Neil J. Leavy S-13
Robert G. LeBlanc S-3
Leon Lebor N-64
Kenneth Charles Ledee N-14
Alan J. Lederman S-60
Elena F. Ledesma N-9
Alexis Leduc S-43
Daniel John Lee N-2
David S. Lee S-42
Dong Chul Lee S-70
Gary H. Lee N-35
Hyun Joon Lee S-48
Juanita Lee S-54
Kathryn Blair Lee N-9
Linda C. Lee N-22
Lorraine Mary Greene Lee S-56
Myoung Woo Lee S-47
Richard Y.C. Lee N-29
Stuart Soo-Jin Lee N-21
Yang Der Lee N-70
Stephen Paul Lefkowitz S-48
Adriana Legro N-61
Edward Joseph Lehman S-54
Eric Lehrfeld N-22
David R. Leistman N-39
David Prudencio Lemagne S-29
Joseph Anthony Lenihan S-34
John Joseph Lennon, Jr. S-28
John Robinson Lenoir S-52
Jorge Luis León, Sr. N-35
Matthew G. Leonard N-46
Michael Lepore N-13
Charles A. Lesperance N-71
Jeff LeVeen N-26
John Dennis Levi S-29

Alisha Caren Levin S-44
Neil David Levin N-65
Robert Levine N-39
Robert Michael Levine S-37
Shai Levinhar N-29
Daniel M. Lewin N-75
Adam Jay Lewis S-35
Jennifer Lewis S-69
Kenneth E. Lewis S-69
Margaret Susan Lewis N-66
Ye Wei Liang N-8
Orasri Liangthanasarn N-69
Daniel F. Libretti S-17
Ralph Michael Licciardi S-64
Edward Lichtschein N-36
Samantha L. Lightbourn-Allen S-76
Steven Barry Lillianthal N-56
Carlos R. Lillo S-11
Craig Damian Lilore N-25
Arnold Arboleda Lim S-41
Darya Lin S-63
Wei Rong Lin N-67
Nickie L. Lindo N-58
Thomas V. Linehan, Jr. N-12
Robert Thomas Linnane S-12
Alan Patrick Linton, Jr. S-52
Diane Theresa Lipari N-61
Kenneth P. Lira Arévalo S-45
Francisco Alberto Liriano N-58
Lorraine Lisi S-40
Paul Lisson S-49
Vincent M. Litto N-25
Ming-Hao Liu S-64
Nancy Liz S-56
Harold Lizcano N-59
Martin Lizzul N-36
George A. Llanes N-63
Elizabeth C. Logler N-34
Catherine Lisa Loguidice N-55
Jérôme Robert Lohez N-65
Michael William Lomax S-57
Stephen V. Long S-73
Laura Maria Longing N-8
Salvatore P. Lopes S-53
Daniel Lopez N-62
George Lopez S-41
Luis Manuel Lopez S-37
Maclovio Lopez, Jr. S-3
Manuel L. Lopez N-14
Joseph Lostrangio N-17
Chet Dek Louie N-46
Stuart Seid Louis S-50
Joseph Lovero S-29
Sara Elizabeth Low N-74
Jenny Seu Kueng Low Wong N-14
Michael W. Lowe S-46
Garry W. Lozier S-52
John P. Lozowsky N-17

Charles Peter Lucania S-64
Edward Hobbs Luckett N-55
Mark Gavin Ludvigsen S-36
Lee Charles Ludwig S-42
Sean Thomas Lugano S-35
Daniel Lugo S-65
Marie Lukas N-35
William Lum, Jr. N-18
Michael P. Lunden N-53
Christopher E. Lunder N-42
Anthony Luparello S-37
Gary Frederick Lutnick N-38
Linda Anne Luzzicone N-45
Alexander Lygin N-48
CeeCee Lyles S-67
Farrell Peter Lynch N-57
James Francis Lynch S-28
James T. Lynch, Jr. S-73
Louise A. Lynch N-15
Michael Cameron Lynch N-41
Michael Francis Lynch S-15
Michael Francis Lynch S-9
Richard D. Lynch, Jr. S-31
Robert Henry Lynch, Jr. S-26
Sean P. Lynch N-26
Sean Patrick Lynch N-57
Terence M. Lynch S-75
Michael J. Lyons S-13
Monica Anne Lyons N-0
Nehamon Lyons IV S-72
Patrick John Lyons S-23
M Robert Francis Mace N-47
Marianne MacFarlane S-2
Jan Maciejewski N-69
Susan A. Mackay N-1
William Macko N-73
Catherine Fairfax MacRae N-59
Richard Blaine Madden S-58
Simon Maddison N-31
Noell C. Maerz S-30
Jennieann Maffeo N-73
Joseph Maffeo S-9
Jay Robert Magazine N-71
Brian Magee N-20
Charles W. Magee N-63
Joseph V. Maggitti N-4
Ronald Magnuson N-48
Daniel L. Maher N-13
Thomas A. Mahon N-51
William J. Mahoney S-11
Joseph Daniel Maio N-30
Linda C. Mair-Grayling N-8
Takashi Makimoto S-44
Abdu Ali Malahi S-45
Debora I. Maldonado N-0
Myrna T. Maldonado-Agosto N-66
Alfred Russell Maler N-54
Gregory James Malone S-32

Edward Francis Maloney III N-50
Joseph E. Maloney S-7
Gene Edward Maloy N-3
Christian H. Maltby N-44
Francisco Miguel Mancini N-71
Joseph Mangano N-3
Sara Elizabeth Manley N-59
Debra M. Mannetta N-61
Marion Victoria Manning N-13
Terence John Manning N-21
James Maounis S-40
Alfred Gilles Padre Joseph
Marchand S-2
Joseph Ross Marchbanks, Jr. S-5
Laura A. Marchese N-65
Hilda Marcin S-67
Peter Edward Mardikian N-21
Edward Joseph Mardovich S-33
Charles Joseph Margiotta S-16
Louis Neil Mariani S-4
Kenneth Joseph Marino S-9
Lester V. Marino N-24
Vita Marino S-51
Kevin D. Marlo S-50
Jose Juan Marrero S-32
John Daniel Marshall S-15
Shelley A. Marshall S-71
James Martello N-26
Michael A. Marti N-51
Karen Ann Martin N-74
Peter C. Martin S-18
Teresa M. Martin S-75
William J. Martin, Jr. N-51
Brian E. Martineau S-62
Betsy Martinez N-32
Edward J. Martinez N-35
Jose Angel Martinez, Jr. N-24
Robert Gabriel Martinez S-65
Waleska Martinez S-67
Lizie D. Martinez-Calderon S-55
Paul Richard Martini S-12
Anne Marie Martino-Cramer S-42
Joseph A. Mascali S-6
Bernard Mascarenhas N-7
Stephen Frank Masi N-35
Ada L. Mason-Acker S-1
Nicholas George Massa S-53
Michael Massaroli N-32
Philip William Mastrandrea, Jr. N-30
Rudy Mastrocinque N-5
Joseph Mathai N-21
Charles William Mathers N-4
William A. Mathesen S-32
Marcello Matricciano N-36
Margaret Elaine Mattic N-72
Dean E. Mattson S-74
Robert D. Mattson S-40
Walter A. Matuza, Jr. N-63

Timothy J. Maude S-74
Jill Maurer-Campbell S-37
Charles A. Mauro, Jr. S-56
Charles J. Mauro N-68
Dorothy Mauro N-9
Nancy T. Mauro N-8
Robert J. Maxwell S-1
Renée A. May and her unborn child S-69
Tyrone May S-48
Keithroy Marcellus Maynard S-14
Robert J. Mayo S-23
Kathy N. Mazza S-29
Edward Mazzella, Jr. N-28
Jennifer Lynn Mazzotta N-33
Kaaria Mbaya N-37
James Joseph McAlary, Jr. N-61
Brian Gerard McAleese S-15
Patricia Ann McAneney N-8
Colin R. McArthur S-58
John Kevin McAvoy S-6
Kenneth M. McBrayer S-52
Brendan F. McCabe S-43
Michael McCabe N-28
Thomas Joseph McCann S-14
Justin McCarthy N-30
Kevin M. McCarthy N-40
Michael Desmond McCarthy N-60
Robert G. McCarthy N-27
Stanley McCaskill N-16
Katie Marie McCloskey N-17
Juliana Valentine McCourt S-3
Ruth Magdaline McCourt S-3
Charles Austin McCrann N-12
Tonyell F. McDay N-13
Matthew T. McDermott N-30
Joseph P. McDonald N-45
Brian Grady McDonnell S-24
Michael P. McDonnell S-36
John F. McDowell, Jr. S-51
Eamon J. McEneaney N-57
John Thomas McErlean, Jr. N-39
Daniel Francis McGinley S-35
Mark Ryan McGinly N-60
William E. McGinn S-21
Thomas Henry McGinnis N-61
Michael Gregory McGinty N-4
Ann Walsh McGovern S-55
Scott Martin McGovern S-31
William J. McGovern S-6
Stacey Sennas McGowan S-51
Francis Noel McGuinn N-51
Thomas F. McGuinness, Jr. N-74
Patrick J. McGuire S-30
Thomas M. McHale S-56
Keith David McHeffey N-28
Ann M. McHugh S-30
Denis J. McHugh III S-33
Dennis P. McHugh S-18

Michael Edward McHugh, Jr. N-34
Robert G. McIlvaine N-22
Donald James McIntyre S-30
Stephanie Marie McKenna N-18
Molly L. McKenzie S-75
Barry J. McKeon S-40
Evelyn C. McKinnedy S-37
Darryl Leron McKinney N-29
George Patrick McLaughlin, Jr. N-59
Robert C. McLaughlin, Jr. N-52
Gavin McMahon S-59
Robert D. McMahon S-13
Edmund M. McNally S-43
Daniel Walker McNeal S-51
Walter Arthur McNeil S-28
Christine Sheila McNulty N-19
Sean Peter McNulty N-28
Robert William McPadden S-15
Terence A. McShane S-9
Timothy Patrick McSweeney S-7
Martin E. McWilliams S-17
Rocco A. Medaglia N-71
Abigail Medina N-16
Ana Iris Medina S-54
Damian Meehan N-61
William J. Meehan, Jr. N-27
Alok Kumar Mehta N-34
Raymond Meisenheimer S-14
Manuel Emilio Mejia N-69
Eskedar Melaku N-14
Antonio Melendez N-70
Mary P. Melendez S-43
Christopher D. Mello N-75
Yelena Melnichenko N-10
Stuart Todd Meltzer N-50
Diarelia Jovanah Mena N-27
Dora Marie Menchaca S-69
Charles R. Mendez S-20
Lizette Mendoza S-60
Shevonne Olicia Mentis N-7
Wolfgang Peter Menzel S-3
Steve John Mercado S-16
Wilfredo Mercado N-73
Wesley Mercer S-47
Ralph Joseph Mercurio N-50
Alan Harvey Merdinger N-0
George L. Merino S-42
Yamel Josefina Merino S-26
George Merkouris N-60
Deborah Merrick N-66
Raymond Joseph Metz III S-32
Jill Ann Metzler S-62
David Robert Meyer N-41
Nurul H. Miah N-15
William Edward Micciulli N-29
Martin Paul Michelstein S-63
Patricia E. Mickley S-71
Ronald D. Milam S-73

Peter Teague Milano N-40
Gregory Milanowycz S-58
Lukasz Tomasz Milewski N-23
Sharon Christina Millan S-45
Corey Peter Miller N-31
Craig J. Miller S-27
Douglas C. Miller S-6
Henry Alfred Miller, Jr. S-20
Joel Miller N-16
Michael Matthew Miller N-55
Nicole Carol Miller S-67
Philip D. Miller S-58
Robert Alan Miller S-48
Robert Cromwell Miller, Jr. S-61
Benny Millman S-64
Charles M. Mills, Jr. S-26
Ronald Keith Milstein S-39
Robert J. Minara S-22
William George Minardi N-54
Louis Joseph Minervino N-15
Thomas Mingione S-22
Wilbert Miraille N-31
Domenick N. Mircovich S-31
Rajesh Arjan Mirpuri N-21
Joseph D. Mistrulli N-71
Susan J. Miszkowicz N-66
Paul Thomas Mitchell S-20
Richard P. Miuccio S-47
Jeffrey Peter Mladenik N-1
Frank V. Moccia, Sr. S-65
Louis Joseph Modafferi S-6
Boyie Mohammed N-62
Dennis Mojica S-8
Manuel D. Mojica, Jr. S-21
Kleber Rolando Molina S-43
Manuel De Jesus Molina N-64
Carl Molinaro S-17
Justin John Molisani, Jr. S-30
Brian Patrick Monaghan S-64
Franklyn Monahan N-32
John Gerard Monahan N-33
Kristen Leigh Montanaro N-3
Craig Montano N-42
Michael G. Montesi S-9
Carlos Alberto Montoya N-75
Antonio De Jesus Montoya Valdes N-74
Cheryl Ann Monyak N-9
Thomas Carlo Moody S-18
Sharon Moore S-52
Krishna V. Moorthy S-43
Laura Lee Defazio Morabito N-75
Abner Morales S-41
Carlos Manuel Morales N-31
Paula E. Morales S-59
Sonia Mercedes Morales Puopolo N-76
Gerard P. Moran, Jr. S-73
John Christopher Moran N-20
John Michael Moran S-11

Kathleen Moran S-63
Lindsay Stapleton Morehouse S-36
George William Morell N-54
Steven P. Morello N-3
Vincent S. Morello S-16
Yvette Nicole Moreno N-59
Dorothy Morgan N-15
Richard J. Morgan S-30
Nancy Morgenstern N-31
Sanae Mori N-22
Blanca Robertina Morocho Morocho N-68
Leonel Geronimo Morocho Morocho N-68
Dennis Gerard Moroney N-47
Lynne Irene Morris N-33
Odessa V. Morris S-76
Seth Allan Morris N-54
Steve Morris N-19
Christopher Martel Morrison N-23
Ferdinand V. Morrone S-27
William David Moskal N-3
Brian A. Moss S-71
Marco Motroni N-62
Cynthia Motus-Wilson N-67
Iouri A. Mouchinski N-71
Jude Joseph Moussa N-50
Peter Moutos N-9
Damion O'Neil Mowatt N-23
Teddington H. Moy S-1
Christopher Michael Mozzillo S-7
Stephen Vincent Mulderry S-33
Richard T. Muldowney, Jr. S-21
Michael D. Mullan S-17
Dennis Michael Mulligan S-17
Peter James Mulligan N-29
Michael Joseph Mullin N-26
James Donald Munhall S-52
Nancy Muñiz N-65
Francisco Heladio Munoz N-4
Carlos Mario Muñoz N-70
Theresa Munson S-57
Robert Michael Murach N-47
Cesar Augusto Murillo N-29
Marc A. Murolo N-53
Brian Joseph Murphy N-55
Charles Anthony Murphy N-56
Christopher W. Murphy S-33
Edward Charles Murphy N-50
James F. Murphy IV N-23
James Thomas Murphy N-54
Kevin James Murphy N-5
Patrick Jude Murphy S-73
Patrick Sean Murphy N-5
Raymond E. Murphy S-19
Robert Eddie Murphy, Jr. S-45
John Joseph Murray N-45
John Joseph Murray S-45
Susan D. Murray N-14
Valerie Victoria Murray N-64

Richard Todd Myhre N-33
Louis J. Nacke II S-68
Robert B. Nagel S-10
Mildred Rose Naiman N-75
Takuya Nakamura N-63
Alexander John Robert Napier S-54
Frank Joseph Naples III N-45
John Philip Napolitano S-17
Catherine Ann Nardella S-61
Mario Nardone, Jr. S-30
Manika K. Narula N-33
Shawn M. Nassaney S-3
Narender Nath N-11
Karen Susan Navarro N-62
Joseph M. Navas S-28
Francis Joseph Nazario N-32
Glenroy I. Neblett N-18
Rayman Marcus Neblett S-60
Jerome O. Nedd N-71
Laurence F. Nedell S-58
Luke G. Nee N-43
Pete Negron S-0
Laurie Ann Neira N-76
Ann N. Nelson N-42
David William Nelson N-61
Ginger Risco Nelson N-60
James A. Nelson S-30
Michele Ann Nelson N-49
Peter Allen Nelson S-12
Oscar Francis Nesbitt S-47
Gerard Terence Nevins S-8
Renee Tetreault Newell N-74
Christopher C. Newton S-71
Christopher Newton-Carter S-51
Nancy Yuen Ngo N-17
Khang Ngoc Nguyen S-73
Jody Tepedino Nichilo N-47
Kathleen Ann Nicosia N-74
Martin Stewart Niederer N-26
Alfonse Joseph Niedermeyer S-28
Frank John Niestadt, Jr. S-62
Gloria Nieves S-40
Juan Nieves, Jr. N-70
Troy Edward Nilsen N-35
Paul Nimbley N-30
John Ballantine Niven S-61
Katherine McGarry Noack N-22
Curtis Terrance Noel N-72
Michael A. Noeth S-72
Daniel R. Nolan N-3
Robert Walter Noonan N-49
Jacqueline June Norton N-2
Robert Grant Norton N-2
Daniela Rosalia Notaro N-58
Brian Christopher Novotny N-45
Soichi Numata S-44
Brian Nunez N-45
Jose Nunez N-71

Jeffrey Roger Nussbaum N-62
Dennis Patrick O'Berg S-20
James P. O'Brien, Jr. N-55
Michael P. O'Brien N-43
Scott J. O'Brien N-22
Timothy Michael O'Brien N-57
Daniel O'Callaghan S-10
Dennis James O'Connor, Jr. N-30
Diana J. O'Connor S-49
Keith Kevin O'Connor S-34
Richard J. O'Connor N-12
Amy O'Doherty N-39
Marni Pont O'Doherty S-36
James Andrew O'Grady S-50
Thomas G. O'Hagan S-13
Patrick J. O'Keefe S-10
William O'Keefe S-11
Gerald Thomas O'Leary N-27
Matthew Timothy O'Mahony N-57
John P. O'Neill N-63
Peter J. O'Neill, Jr. S-52
Sean Gordon Corbett O'Neill N-25
Kevin M. O'Rourke S-17
Patrick J. O'Shea N-61
Robert William O'Shea N-60
Timothy Franklin O'Sullivan N-73
James A. Oakley N-9
Douglas E. Oelschlager S-20
Takashi Ogawa N-22
Albert Ogletree N-24
Philip Paul Ognibene S-36
John A. Ogonowski N-74
Joseph J. Ogren S-7
Samuel Oitice S-9
Gerald Michael Olcott N-11
Christine Anne Olender N-68
Linda Mary Oliva N-59
Edward K. Oliver N-61
Leah Elizabeth Oliver N-12
Eric Taube Olsen S-20
Jeffrey James Olsen S-5
Barbara K. Olson S-70
Maureen Lyons Olson N-7
Steven John Olson S-8
Toshihiro Onda S-44
Seamus L. Oneal N-37
Betty Ann Ong N-74
Michael C. Opperman S-61
Christopher T. Orgielewicz S-49
Margaret Quinn Orloske N-8
Virginia Anne Ormiston N-5
Ruben S. Ornedo S-70
Ronald Orsini N-56
Peter Keith Ortale S-33
Juan Ortega-Campos S-38
Jane Marie Orth N-75
Alexander Ortiz N-65
David Ortiz S-27

Emilio Pete Ortiz N-62
Pablo Ortiz N-67
Paul Ortiz, Jr. N-21
Sonia Ortiz N-64
Masaru Ose S-44
Elsy Carolina Osorio Oliva N-72
James R. Ostrowski N-46
Jason Douglas Oswald N-48
Michael John Otten S-16
Isidro D. Ottenwalder N-68
Michael Chung Ou S-48
Todd Joseph Ouida N-44
Jesus Ovalles N-69
Peter J. Owens, Jr. N-42
Adianes Oyola S-45
Angel M. Pabon, Jr. N-28
Israel Pabon, Jr. N-24
Roland Pacheco N-65
Michael Benjamin Packer N-22
Diana B. Padro S-76
Deepa Pakkala N-17
Jeffrey Matthew Palazzo S-5
Thomas Palazzo N-54
Richard A. Palazzolo N-54
Orio Joseph Palmer S-17
Frank Anthony Palombo S-21
Alan N. Palumbo N-51
Christopher Matthew Panatier N-45
Dominique Lisa Pandolfo N-14
Jonas Martin Panik S-73
Paul J. Pansini S-5
John M. Paolillo S-11
Edward Joseph Papa N-54
Salvatore T. Papasso S-26
James Nicholas Pappageorge S-14
Marie Pappalardo S-2
Vinod Kumar Parakat N-29
Vijayashanker Paramsothy S-57
Nitin Ramesh Parandkar N-19
Hardai Parbhu S-56
James Wendell Parham S-29
Debra Marie Paris S-53
George Paris N-33
Gye Hyong Park N-64
Philip Lacey Parker S-61
Michael Alaine Parkes N-12
Robert E. Parks, Jr. N-46
Hashmukh C. Parmar N-37
Robert Parro S-16
Diane Marie Parsons S-47
Leobardo Lopez Pascual N-70
Michael J. Pascuma, Jr. N-67
Jerrold Hughes Paskins N-17
Horace Robert Passananti N-11
Suzanne H. Passaro S-53
Avnish Ramanbhai Patel N-59
Dipti Patel N-33
Manish Patel S-30

Steven Bennett Paterson N-51
James Matthew Patrick N-51
Manuel D. Patrocino N-70
Bernard E. Patterson N-43
Clifford L. Patterson, Jr. S-74
Cira Marie Patti S-34
Robert E. Pattison N-63
James Robert Paul N-60
Patrice Paz S-61
Victor Hugo Paz N-69
Stacey Lynn Peak N-50
Richard Allen Pearlman S-27
Durrell V. Pearsall, Jr. S-11
Thomas Nicholas Pecorelli N-74
Thomas Pedicini N-42
Todd Douglas Pelino N-54
Mike Adrian Pelletier N-49
Anthony G. Peluso S-36
Angel R. Pena S-56
Robert Penninger S-69
Richard Al Penny S-49
Salvatore F. Pepe N-3
Carl Allen B. Peralta N-30
Robert David Peraza N-32
Jon A. Perconti, Jr. N-27
Alejo Perez N-67
Angel Perez, Jr. N-33
Angela Susan Perez N-32
Anthony Perez N-37
Ivan Antonio Perez S-41
Nancy E. Perez N-66
Berry Berenson Perkins N-76
Joseph John Perroncino N-32
Edward J. Perrotta N-50
Emelda H. Perry S-64
Glenn C. Perry, Sr. S-22
John William Perry S-24
Franklin Allan Pershep S-56
Danny Pesce N-55
Michael John Pescherine S-34
Davin N. Peterson N-28
Donald Arthur Peterson S-67
Jean Hoadley Peterson S-67
William Russell Peterson N-15
Mark James Petrocelli N-61
Philip Scott Petti S-16
Glen Kerrin Pettit S-25
Dominick A. Pezzulo S-29
Kaleen Elizabeth Pezzuti N-54
Kevin J. Pfeifer S-14
Tu-Anh Pham N-60
Kenneth John Phelan, Sr. S-13
Sneha Anne Philip S-66
Eugenia McCann Piantieri N-13
Ludwig John Picarro S-63
Matthew Picerno N-43
Joseph O. Pick S-41
Christopher J. Pickford S-12

Dennis J. Pierce S-47
Bernard Pietronico N-41
Nicholas P. Pietrunti N-30
Theodoros Pigis S-49
Susan Elizabeth Pinto N-35
Joseph Piskadlo N-63
Christopher Todd Pitman N-45
Joshua Michael Piver N-33
Robert R. Ploger III S-71
Zandra F. Ploger S-71
Joseph Plumitallo N-41
John M. Pocher N-41
William Howard Pohlmann S-47
Laurence Michael Polatsch N-27
Thomas H. Polhemus N-17
Steve Pollicino N-39
Susan M. Pollio S-33
Darin H. Pontell S-73
Joshua Iosua Poptean N-71
Giovanna Porras N-72
Anthony Portillo S-49
James Edward Potorti N-11
Daphne Pouletsos S-55
Richard N. Poulos N-30
Stephen Emanual Poulos S-60
Brandon Jerome Powell N-23
Scott Alan Powell S-75
Shawn Edward Powell S-20
Antonio Dorsey Pratt N-23
Gregory M. Preziose N-53
Wanda Ivelisse Prince S-42
Vincent A. Princiotta S-20
Kevin M. Prior S-22
Everett Martin Proctor III N-48
Carrie Beth Progen S-59
David Lee Pruim S-62
Richard A. Prunty S-5
John Foster Puckett N-68
Robert David Pugliese N-10
Edward F. Pullis S-62
Patricia Ann Puma N-64
Jack D. Punches S-73
Hemanth Kumar Puttur N-17
Joseph J. Pycior, Jr. S-72
Edward R. Pykon N-61
Christopher Quackenbush S-52
Lars Peter Qualben N-15
Lincoln Quappé S-16
Beth Ann Quigley N-27
Patrick J. Quigley IV S-4
Michael T. Quilty S-15
James Francis Quinn N-30
Ricardo J. Quinn S-18
Carol Millicent Rabalais S-61
Christopher Peter Anthony
Racaniello N-32
Leonard J. Ragaglia S-10
Eugene J. Raggio S-24

Laura Marie Ragonese-Snik S-54
Michael Paul Ragusa S-23
Peter Frank Raimondi N-59
Harry A. Raines N-36
Lisa J. Raines S-71
Ehtesham Raja S-39
Valsa Raju N-63
Edward J. Rall S-17
Lukas Rambousek N-58
Maria Ramirez S-45
Harry Ramos N-63
Vishnoo Ramsaroop N-64
Deborah A. Ramsaur S-1
Lorenzo E. Ramzey S-55
Alfred Todd Rancke S-50
Adam David Rand S-8
Jonathan C. Randall N-6
Shreyas S. Ranganath N-7
Anne T. Ransom N-18
Faina Rapoport N-17
Rhonda Sue Rasmussen S-76
Robert A. Rasmussen S-37
Amenia Rasool N-11
R. Mark Rasweiler N-9
Marsha D. Ratchford S-72
David Alan James Rathkey S-46
William Ralph Raub N-25
Gerard F. Rauzi S-47
Alexey Razuvaev S-32
Gregory Reda N-6
Sarah Anne Redheffer N-20
Michele Marie Reed S-62
Judith Ann Reese N-67
Donald J. Regan S-14
Robert M. Regan S-10
Thomas Michael Regan S-54
Christian Michael Otto Regenhard S-23
Howard Reich S-49
Gregg Reidy N-28
James Brian Reilly S-34
Kevin O. Reilly S-20
Timothy E. Reilly N-11
Joseph Reina, Jr. N-33
Thomas Barnes Reinig N-55
Frank Bennett Reisman N-28
Joshua Scott Reiss N-51
Karen Renda N-18
John Armand Reo N-40
Richard Cyril Rescorla S-46
John Thomas Resta N-62
Sylvia San Pio Resta and her
unborn child N-62
Martha M. Reszke S-1
David E. Retik N-1
Todd H. Reuben S-69
Luis Clodoaldo Revilla Mier S-65
Eduvigis Reyes, Jr. N-72
Bruce Albert Reynolds S-28

John Frederick Rhodes S-55
Francis Saverio Riccardelli S-25
Rudolph N. Riccio N-34
Ann Marie Riccoboni N-64
David Harlow Rice S-52
Eileen Mary Rice N-6
Kenneth Frederick Rice III N-13
CeCelia E. Richard S-76
Vernon Allan Richard S-20
Claude Daniel Richards S-25
Gregory David Richards N-39
Michael Richards N-63
Venesha Orintia Richards N-6
Jimmy Riches S-21
Alan Jay Richman N-11
John M. Rigo N-10
Frederick Charles Rimmele III S-2
Rose Mary Riso S-47
Moises N. Rivas N-67
Joseph R. Rivelli, Jr. S-22
Carmen Alicia Rivera S-42
Isaias Rivera N-63
Juan William Rivera N-72
Linda Ivelisse Rivera N-15
David E. Rivers N-20
Joseph R. Riverso N-51
Paul V. Rizza S-40
John Frank Rizzo S-64
Stephen Louis Roach N-54
Joseph Roberto S-35
Leo Arthur Roberts N-43
Michael E. Roberts S-21
Michael Edward Roberts S-16
Donald Walter Robertson, Jr. N-45
Jeffrey Robinson N-16
Michell Lee Jean Robotham S-56
Donald Arthur Robson N-39
Antonio A. Rocha N-51
Raymond James Rocha N-44
Laura Rockefeller N-20
John Michael Rodak S-51
Antonio José Rodrigues S-29
Anthony Rodriguez S-22
Carmen Milagros Rodriguez S-58
Gregory E. Rodriguez N-48
Marsha A. Rodriguez N-6
Mayra Valdes Rodriguez S-59
Richard Rodriguez S-29
David Bartolo Rodriguez-Vargas N-69
Matthew Rogan S-14
Jean Destrehan Rogér N-74
Karlie Rogers N-20
Scott William Rohner N-44
Keith Michael Roma S-25
Joseph M. Romagnolo N-24
Efrain Romero, Sr. S-44
Elvin Romero N-28
James A. Romito S-27

Sean Paul Rooney S-57
Eric Thomas Ropiteau N-33
Aida Rosario N-18
Angela Rosario N-29
Mark H. Rosen S-52
Brooke David Rosenbaum N-33
Linda Rosenbaum N-12
Sheryl Lynn Rosenbaum N-47
Lloyd Daniel Rosenberg N-40
Mark Louis Rosenberg N-7
Andrew Ira Rosenblum N-40
Joshua M. Rosenblum N-27
Joshua Alan Rosenthal S-41
Richard David Rosenthal N-48
Philip Martin Rosenzweig N-2
Daniel Rosetti S-64
Richard Barry Ross N-2
Norman S. Rossinow S-61
Nicholas P. Rossomando S-5
Michael Craig Rothberg N-29
Donna Marie Rothenberg S-60
Mark David Rothenberg S-68
James Michael Roux S-2
Nicholas Charles Alexander Rowe N-23
Edward V. Rowenhorst S-76
Judy Rowlett S-1
Timothy Alan Roy, Sr. S-24
Paul G. Ruback S-21
Ronald J. Ruben S-34
Joanne Rubino N-14
David M. Ruddle S-66
Bart Joseph Ruggiere N-49
Susan A. Ruggiero N-13
Adam Keith Ruhalter N-47
Gilbert Ruiz N-69
Robert E. Russell S-1
Stephen P. Russell S-7
Steven Harris Russin N-52
Michael Thomas Russo, Sr. S-7
Wayne Alan Russo N-6
William R. Ruth S-74
Edward Ryan N-61
John Joseph Ryan S-34
Jonathan Stephan Ryan S-30
Matthew L. Ryan S-9
Tatiana Ryjova S-48
Christina Sunga Ryook N-49
Thierry Saada N-41
Jason Elazar Sabbag S-42
Thomas E. Sabella S-17
Scott H. Saber N-23
Charles E. Sabin, Sr. S-71
Joseph Francis Sacerdote N-44
Jessica Leigh Sachs N-74
Francis John Sadocha N-24
Jude Elias Safi N-26
Brock Joel Safronoff N-7
Edward Saiya S-45

John Patrick Salamone N-40
Marjorie C. Salamone S-75
Hernando Rafael Salas S-38
Juan G. Salas N-70
Esmerlin Antonio Salcedo S-65
John Pepe Salerno N-30
Rahma Salie and her unborn child N-1
Richard L. Salinardi, Jr. S-37
Wayne John Saloman N-35
Nolbert Salomon S-46
Catherine Patricia Salter S-60
Frank G. Salvaterra S-51
Paul Richard Salvio N-62
Samuel Robert Salvo, Jr. S-59
Carlos Alberto Samaniego N-42
John P. Sammartino S-71
James Kenneth Samuel, Jr. N-60
Michael San Phillip S-51
Hugo M. Sanay S-31
Alva Cynthia Jeffries Sanchez N-16
Jacquelyn Patrice Sanchez N-47
Jesus Sanchez S-2
Raymond Sanchez S-66
Eric M. Sand N-28
Stacey Leigh Sanders N-3
Herman S. Sandler S-52
Jim Sands, Jr. N-36
Ayleen J. Santiago N-65
Kirsten Reese Santiago N-67
Maria Theresa Concepcion
Santillan N-36
Susan Gayle Santo N-9
Christopher A. Santora S-10
John August Santore S-5
Mario L. Santoro S-26
Rafael Humberto Santos N-34
Rufino C.F. Santos III N-17
Victor J. Saracini S-2
Kalyan K. Sarkar N-66
Chapelle Renee Stewart Sarker N-14
Paul F. Sarle N-56
Deepika Kumar Sattaluri N-18
Gregory Thomas Saucedo S-6
Susan M. Sauer N-11
Anthony Savas N-67
Vladimir Savinkin N-48
John Michael Sbarbaro N-56
David M. Scales S-74
Robert Louis Scandole N-52
Michelle Scarpitta S-31
Dennis Scauso S-8
John Albert Schardt S-12
John G. Scharf S-63
Fred C. Scheffold, Jr. S-6
Angela Susan Scheinberg N-64
Scott Mitchell Schertzer N-33
Sean Schielke N-44
Steven Francis Schlag N-51

Robert A. Schlegel S-72
Jon Schlissel S-48
Karen Helene Schmidt S-46
Ian Schneider N-52
Thomas G. Schoales S-21
Marisa Dinardo Schorpp N-49
Frank G. Schott, Jr. N-13
Gerard Patrick Schrang S-14
Jeffrey H. Schreier N-31
John T. Schroeder N-59
Susan Lee Schuler S-53
Edward W. Schunk N-55
Mark Evan Schurmeier N-22
John Burkhart Schwartz N-40
Mark Schwartz S-26
Adriane Victoria Scibetta N-48
Raphael Scorca N-3
Janice M. Scott S-1
Randolph Scott S-31
Christopher Jay Scudder S-37
Arthur Warren Scullin N-14
Michael H. Seaman N-46
Margaret M. Seeliger S-53
Anthony Segarra N-64
Carlos Segarra N-72
Jason M. Sekzer N-31
Matthew Carmen Sellitto N-46
Michael L. Selves S-75
Howard Selwyn S-31
Larry John Senko N-65
Arturo Angelo Sereno N-58
Frankie Serrano S-45
Marian H. Serva S-75
Alena Sesinova N-3
Adele Christine Sessa N-27
Sita Nermalla Sewnarine S-43
Karen Lynn Seymour N-73
Davis Grier Sezna, Jr. S-52
Thomas Joseph Sgroi N-8
Jayesh Shantilal Shah S-37
Khalid M. Shahid N-33
Mohammed Shajahan N-14
Gary Shamay N-31
Earl Richard Shanahan N-5
Dan F. Shanower S-72
Neil G. Shastri N-58
Kathryn Anne Shatzoff N-10
Barbara A. Shaw N-20
Jeffrey James Shaw N-24
Robert John Shay, Jr. N-53
Daniel James Shea N-38
Joseph Patrick Shea N-38
Kathleen Shearer S-3
Robert M. Shearer S-3
Linda June Sheehan S-50
Hagay Shefi N-21
Antionette M. Sherman S-75
John Anthony Sherry S-30

Atsushi Shiratori N-44
Thomas Joseph Shubert N-29
Mark Shulman N-10
See Wong Shum N-71
Allan Abraham Shwartzstein N-30
Clarin Shellie Siegel-Schwartz S-53
Johanna Sigmund N-60
Dianne T. Signer and her unborn child N-60
Gregory Sikorsky S-12
Stephen Gerard Siller S-5
David Silver N-29
Craig A. Silverstein S-50
Nasima H. Simjee S-41
Bruce Edward Simmons S-51
Diane M. Simmons S-69
Donald D. Simmons S-76
George W. Simmons S-69
Arthur Simon N-58
Kenneth Alan Simon N-58
Michael J. Simon N-49
Paul Joseph Simon N-17
Marianne Liquori Simone N-35
Barry Simowitz S-48
Jane Louise Simpkin S-2
Jeff Lyal Simpson S-27
Cheryle D. Sincock S-75
Khamladai Khami Singh N-68
Roshan Ramesh Singh N-68
Thomas E. Sinton III N-55
Peter A. Siracuse N-39
Muriel F. Siskopoulos S-33
Joseph Michael Sisolak N-6
John P. Skala S-27
Francis Joseph Skidmore, Jr. S-32
Toyena Corliss Skinner N-72
Paul Albert Skrzypek N-50
Christopher Paul Slattery N-30
Vincent Robert Slavin N-27
Robert F. Sliwak N-56
Paul Kenneth Sloan S-33
Stanley S. Smagala, Jr. S-15
Wendy L. Small N-54
Gregg H. Smallwood S-72
Catherine T. Smith N-16
Daniel Laurence Smith S-31
Gary F. Smith S-1
George Eric Smith S-39
Heather Lee Smith N-75
James Gregory Smith N-40
Jeffrey R. Smith S-52
Joyce Patricia Smith N-24
Karl T. Smith, Sr. N-43
Kevin Joseph Smith S-9
Leon Smith, Jr. S-11
Moira Ann Smith S-24
Monica Rodriguez Smith and her unborn child N-73
Rosemary A. Smith N-73

Bonnie Shihadeh Smithwick N-61
Rochelle Monique Snell S-49
Christine Ann Snyder S-67
Dianne Bullis Snyder N-74
Leonard J. Snyder, Jr. S-54
Astrid Elizabeth Sohan N-6
Sushil S. Solanki N-34
Rubén Solares N-31
Naomi Leah Solomon N-21
Daniel W. Song N-56
Mari-Rae Sopper S-69
Michael Charles Sorresse N-5
Fabian Soto N-63
Timothy Patrick Soulas N-44
Gregory Thomas Spagnoletti S-35
Donald F. Spampinato, Jr. N-39
Thomas Sparacio S-32
John Anthony Spataro N-10
Robert W. Spear, Jr. S-19
Robert Speisman S-70
Maynard S. Spence, Jr. N-6
George Edward Spencer III S-31
Robert Andrew Spencer N-45
Mary Rubina Sperando N-21
Frank Spinelli N-44
William E. Spitz N-42
Joseph Patrick Spor, Jr. S-15
Klaus Johannes Sprockamp S-47
Saranya Srinuan N-52
Fitzroy St. Rose N-72
Michael F. Stabile S-32
Lawrence T. Stack S-18
Timothy M. Stackpole S-20
Richard James Stadelberger S-40
Eric Adam Stahlman N-46
Gregory Stajk S-17
Alexandru Liviu Stan N-34
Corina Stan N-34
Mary Domenica Stanley N-14
Anthony Starita N-42
Jeffrey Stark S-13
Derek James Statkevicus S-34
Patricia J. Statz S-75
Craig William Staub S-34
William V. Steckman N-67
Eric Thomas Steen S-30
William R. Steiner N-12
Alexander Robbins Steinman N-25
Edna L. Stephens S-1
Andrew Stergiopoulos N-45
Andrew J. Stern N-43
Norma Lang Steuerle S-69
Martha Jane Stevens S-62
Michael James Stewart N-61
Richard H. Stewart, Jr. N-41
Sanford M. Stoller N-17
Douglas Joel Stone N-74
Lonny Jay Stone N-63

Jimmy Nevill Storey N-12
Timothy Stout N-35
Thomas Strada N-40
James J. Straine, Jr. N-52
Edward W. Straub S-55
George J. Strauch, Jr. S-60
Edward Thomas Strauss S-24
Steven R. Strauss S-46
Larry L. Strickland S-74
Steven F. Strobert N-55
Walwyn Wellington Stuart, Jr. S-29
Benjamin Suarez S-11
David Scott Suarez N-17
Ramon Suarez S-25
Dino Xavier Suarez Ramirez N-75
Yoichi Sumiyama Sugiyama S-44
William Christopher Sugra N-34
Daniel Thomas Suhr S-14
David Marc Sullins S-25
Christopher P. Sullivan S-22
Patrick Sullivan N-40
Thomas G. Sullivan N-67
Hilario Soriano Sumaya, Jr. N-8
James Joseph Suozzo N-41
Colleen M. Supinski S-51
Robert Sutcliffe N-67
Seline Sutter N-65
Claudia Suzette Sutton N-48
John Francis Swaine N-39
Kristine M. Swearson N-34
Brian David Sweeney S-2
Brian Edward Sweeney S-9
Madeline Amy Sweeney N-74
Kenneth J. Swenson N-48
Thomas F. Swift S-46
Derek Ogilvie Sword S-35
Kevin Thomas Szocik S-35
Gina Sztejnberg N-15
Norbert P. Szurkowski N-50
Harry Taback N-4
Joann C. Tabeek N-35
Norma C. Taddei N-13
Michael Taddonio S-31
Keiichiro Takahashi S-32
Keiji Takahashi S-44
Phyllis Gail Talbot N-11
Robert R. Talhami N-27
John Talignani S-68
Sean Patrick Tallon S-5
Paul Talty S-24
Maurita Tam S-53
Rachel Tamares S-61
Hector Rogan Tamayo S-45
Michael Andrew Tamuccio N-59
Kenichiro Tanaka S-44
Rhondelle Cherie Tankard S-59
Michael Anthony Tanner N-25
Dennis Gerard Taormina, Jr. N-12

Kenneth Joseph Tarantino N-46
Allan Tarasiewicz S-7
Michael C. Tarrou S-2
Ronald Tartaro N-60
Deborah Tavolarella S-2
Darryl Anthony Taylor N-72
Donnie Brooks Taylor S-59
Hilda E. Taylor S-70
Kip P. Taylor S-74
Leonard E. Taylor S-71
Lorisa Ceylon Taylor N-15
Michael Morgan Taylor N-40
Sandra C. Taylor S-1
Sandra Dawn Teague S-69
Karl W. Teepe S-71
Paul A. Tegtmeier S-21
Yeshavant Moreshwar Tembe S-47
Anthony Tempesta N-53
Dorothy Pearl Temple S-47
Stanley L. Temple N-31
David Gustaf Peter Tengelin N-4
Brian John Terrenzi N-47
Lisa Marie Terry N-11
Goumatie Thackurdeen S-41
Harshad Sham Thatte N-17
Michael Theodoridis N-1
Thomas F. Theurkauf, Jr. S-36
Lesley Anne Thomas N-49
Brian Thomas Thompson S-44
Clive Ian Thompson S-32
Glenn Thompson N-43
Nigel Bruce Thompson N-44
Perry A. Thompson S-60
Vanavah Alexei Thompson N-64
William H. Thompson S-26
Eric Raymond Thorpe S-35
Nichola Angela Thorpe S-33
Tamara C. Thurman S-74
Sal Edward Tieri, Jr. N-10
John Patrick Tierney S-13
Mary Ellen Tiesi S-62
William Randolph Tieste N-25
Kenneth Tietjen S-29
Stephen Edward Tighe N-56
Scott Charles Timmes N-62
Michael E. Tinley N-15
Jennifer M. Tino N-11
Robert Frank Tipaldi N-26
John James Tipping II S-10
David Tirado N-23
Hector Luis Tirado, Jr. S-15
Michelle Lee Titolo N-48
Alicia Nicole Titus S-2
John J. Tobin N-8
Richard J. Todisco S-51
Otis V. Tolbert S-73
Vladimir Tomasevic N-22
Stephen Kevin Tompsett N-22

Thomas Tong S-39
Doris Torres S-42
Luis Eduardo Torres N-51
Amy Elizabeth Toyen N-23
Christopher Michael Traina N-63
Daniel Patrick Trant N-43
Abdoul Karim Traore N-68
Glenn J. Travers, Sr. N-32
Walter Philip Travers N-56
Felicia Yvette Traylor-Bass N-65
James Anthony Trentini N-2
Mary Barbara Trentini N-2
Lisa L. Trerotola N-67
Karamo Baba Trerra S-39
Michael Angel Trinidad N-31
Francis Joseph Trombino S-38
Gregory James Trost S-33
Willie Q. Troy S-1
William P. Tselepis, Jr. N-45
Zhanetta Valentinovna Tsoy N-13
Michael Patrick Tucker N-28
Lance Richard Tumulty S-31
Ching Ping Tung S-44
Simon James Turner N-20
Donald Joseph Tuzio S-39
Robert T. Twomey N-67
Jennifer Lynn Tzemis N-58
John G. Ueltzhoeffer N-15
Tyler Victor Ugolyn N-59
Michael A. Uliano N-56
Jonathan J. Uman N-38
Anil Shivhari Umarkar N-34
Allen V. Upton N-39
Diane Marie Urban S-47
John Damien Vaccacio N-43
Bradley Hodges Vadas S-35
William Valcarcel S-48
Felix Antonio Vale N-32
Ivan Vale N-32
Benito Valentin N-18
Santos Valentin, Jr. S-25
Carlton Francis Valvo II N-46
Pendyala Vamsikrishna N-74
Erica H. Van Acker S-55
Kenneth W. Van Auken N-52
R. Bruce Van Hine S-13
Daniel M. Van Laere S-62
Edward Raymond Vanacore S-41
Jon Charles Vandevander N-62
Frederick T. Varacchi N-38
Gopalakrishnan Varadhan N-46
David Vargas S-49
Scott C. Vasel N-16
Azael Ismael Vasquez N-24
Ronald J. Vauk S-73
Arcangel Vazquez S-41
Santos Vazquez N-31
Peter Vega S-11

Sankara Sastry Velamuri S-47
Jorge Velazquez S-47
Lawrence G. Veling S-7
Anthony Mark Ventura S-41
David Vera S-31
Loretta Ann Vero N-18
Christopher James Vialonga N-62
Matthew Gilbert Vianna N-34
Robert Anthony Vicario N-24
Celeste Torres Victoria N-20
Joanna Vidal N-20
John T. Vigiano II S-23
Joseph Vincent Vigiano S-23
Frank J. Vignola, Jr. N-48
Joseph Barry Vilardo N-28
Claribel Villalobos Hernandez N-23
Sergio Gabriel Villanueva S-23
Chantal Vincelli N-21
Melissa Renée Vincent N-65
Francine Ann Virgilio N-61
Lawrence Virgilio S-20
Joseph Gerard Visciano S-34
Joshua S. Vitale N-26
Maria Percoco Vola S-62
Lynette D. Vosges S-59
Garo H. Voskerijian N-13
Alfred Anton Vukosa N-35
Gregory Kamal Bruno Wachtler N-60
Karen J. Wagner S-74
Mary Alice Wahlstrom N-1
Honor Elizabeth Wainio S-67
Gabriela Silvina Waisman N-23
Wendy Alice Rosario Wakeford N-53
Courtney Wainsworth Walcott S-46
Victor Wald N-63
Kenneth E. Waldie N-2
Benjamin James Walker N-16
Glen Wall N-57
Mitchel Scott Wallace S-26
Peter Guyder Wallace N-6
Robert Francis Wallace S-12
Roy Michael Wallace N-44
Jeanmarie Wallendorf S-36
Matthew Blake Wallens N-39
Meta L. Waller S-1
John Wallice, Jr. N-30
Barbara P. Walsh N-9
Jim Walsh N-34
Jeffrey P. Walz S-14
Ching Wang S-44
Weibin Wang N-36
Michael Warchola S-6
Stephen Gordon Ward N-48
Timothy Ray Ward S-2
James A. Waring N-31
Brian G. Warner N-37
Derrick Christopher Washington S-66
Charles Waters N-32

James Thomas Waters, Jr. S-34
Patrick J. Waters S-8
Kenneth Thomas Watson S-21
Michael Henry Waye N-8
Todd Christopher Weaver S-43
Walter Edward Weaver S-25
Nathaniel Webb S-28
Dinah Webster N-20
William Michael Weems S-4
Joanne Flora Weil S-45
Michael T. Weinberg S-17
Steven Weinberg S-37
Scott Jeffrey Weingard N-27
Steven George Weinstein N-13
Simon Weiser N-65
David M. Weiss S-8
David Thomas Weiss N-46
Chin Sun Pak Wells S-74
Vincent Michael Wells N-44
Deborah Jacobs Welsh S-67
Timothy Matthew Welty S-7
Christian Hans Rudolf Wemmers N-21
Ssu-Hui Wen N-34
John Joseph Wenckus N-2
Oleh D. Wengerchuk S-65
Peter M. West N-43
Whitfield West, Jr. N-35
Meredith Lynn Whalen N-60
Eugene Michael Whelan S-12
Adam S. White N-50
Edward James White III S-13
James Patrick White N-39
John Sylvester White N-63
Kenneth Wilburn White, Jr. N-24
Leonard Anthony White S-66
Malissa Y. White N-15
Maudlyn A. White S-74
Sandra L. White S-75
Wayne White N-9
Leanne Marie Whiteside S-59
Mark P. Whitford S-15
Leslie A. Whittington S-69
Michael T. Wholey S-29
Mary Lenz Wieman S-59
Jeffrey David Wiener N-12
William J. Wik S-60
Alison Marie Wildman N-61
Glenn E. Wilkinson S-14
Ernest M. Willcher S-75
John Charles Willett N-50
Brian Patrick Williams N-41
Candace Lee Williams N-75
Crossley Richard Williams, Jr. S-41
David J. Williams N-64
David Lucian Williams S-73
Debbie L. Williams S-54
Dwayne Williams S-74
Kevin Michael Williams S-50

Louie Anthony Williams N-66
Louis Calvin Williams III S-37
John P. Williamson S-8
Donna Ann Wilson S-56
William Eben Wilson S-61
David Harold Winton S-35
Glenn J. Winuk S-27
Thomas Francis Wise N-9
Alan L. Wisniewski S-52
Frank Paul Wisniewski N-53
David Wiswall S-55
Sigrid Charlotte Wiswe N-18
Michael R. Wittenstein N-52
Christopher W. Wodenshek N-49
Martin Phillips Wohlforth S-52
Katherine Susan Wolf N-3
Jennifer Yen Wong N-20
Siucheung Steve Wong N-4
Yin Ping Wong S-60
Yuk Ping Wong S-48
Brent James Woodall S-33
James John Woods N-26
Marvin Roger Woods S-73
Patrick J. Woods S-64
Richard Herron Woodwell S-35
David Terence Wooley S-9
John Bentley Works S-34
Martin Michael Wortley N-46
Rodney James Wotton S-43
William Wren, Ret. S-22
John W. Wright, Jr. S-50
Neil Robin Wright N-46
Sandra Lee Wright S-57
Jupiter Yambem N-69
John D. Yamnicky, Sr. S-71
Suresh Yanamadala N-16
Vicki Yancey S-70
Shuyin Yang S-70
Matthew David Yarnell S-41
Myrna Yaskulka N-60
Shakila Yasmin N-15
Olabisi Shadie Layeni Yee N-67
Kevin W. Yokum S-72
Edward P. York N-49
Kevin Patrick York S-31
Raymond R. York S-20
Suzanne Martha Youmans S-54
Barrington Leroy Young, Jr. S-31
Donald McArthur Young S-72
Edmond G. Young, Jr. S-74
Jacqueline Young N-3
Lisa L. Young S-1
Elkin Yuen N-61
Joseph C. Zaccoli N-43
Adel Agayby Zakhary N-63
Arkady Zaltsman S-63
Edwin J. Zambrana, Jr. S-49
Robert Alan Zampieri N-62

Mark Zangrilli S-63
Christopher R. Zarba, Jr. N-1
Ira Zaslow S-46
Kenneth Albert Zelman N-19
Abraham J. Zelmanowitz N-65
Martin Morales Zempoaltecatl N-68
Zhe Zeng S-37
Marc Scott Zeplin N-27
Jie Yao Justin Zhao S-39
Yuguang Zheng S-70

Ivelin Ziminski N-5
Michael Joseph Zinzi N-14
Charles Alan Zion N-25
Julie Lynne Zipper S-49
Salvatore J. Zisa N-5
Prokopios Paul Zois N-18
Joseph J. Zuccala S-44
Andrew Steven Zucker S-45
Igor Zukelman S-4

Made in the USA
Monee, IL
29 April 2023

32663598R00070